Hot Sonnets

Hot Sonnets

An Anthology

Moira Egan and Clarinda Harriss
Editors

ENTASIS PRESS
WASHINGTON, D.C.

Published by
ENTASIS PRESS
WASHINGTON, D.C.
2011

ISBN 978-0-9800999-9-7

Library of Congress Control Number: 2011923274
Copyright 2011 by Moira Egan and Clarinda Harriss

All rights reserved. No part of this publication may be reproduced, stored in a retrieval system, or transmitted, in any form or by any means, without the prior written permission of the publisher. Printed in the United States. This copyright extends to all rights and permissions noted in the acknowledgments section at the end of this book.

Cover art: *La Boîte à Violon* by Suzanne Valadon
Musée d'Art Moderne de la Ville de Paris
© The Image Works, Inc. Used by permission.

This book was funded in part by Towson University's Clarisse Mechanic English Department Discretionary Fund. The editors would like to express their gratitude to Fabrice Hergott, Ed Perlman, and Louis-Antoine Prat.

This collection is dedicated to all the sonnet lovers who came before us, and all who will come after.

Contents

MOIRA EGAN
Introduction, On Hot Sonnets   25

CLARINDA HARRISS
An editor's note, My Dear Old Sonnet   29
My dear old Sonnet, mother of my muse,

EDNA ST. VINCENT MILLAY
cxxv   31
I too beneath your moon, almighty Sex,
xli   32
I, being born a woman and distressed
xcvii   33
When we are old and these rejoicing veins

E.E. CUMMINGS
xxiv.   34
and this day it was Spring...us
ii.   35
when I have thought of you somewhat too
vii.   36
After your poppied hair inaugurates

JOHN BERRYMAN
Sonnet #1   37
I wished, all the mild days of middle March
Sonnet #4   38
Ah when you drift hover before you kiss

HAYDEN CARRUTH
Sonnet 9   39
To see a woman long oppressed by fear

WILLIS BARNSTONE
With a French Nun in Lapland   40
Even the constant sun wears a small coat

THOM GUNN
Diagrams   41
Downtown, an office tower is going up.

GRACE CAVALIERI
Anna Nicole's Dream   42
A cup of jewels, a star, flying dragons,

WESLI COURT
Sports Harassment Embarrassment 2010   43
The day when Inez Sainz came marching in
Venal Song   44
Hour on hour I've wandered Venus' arbor

MICHAEL CANTOR
The Love of Sushi Sue
#1   45
I lived near Tokyo's Hama-Zushi bar
#2   46
In time, the real-life girlfriends disappeared,
#3   47
Although all that was years ago, the quest

CLARINDA HARRISS
Thunder   48
They also serve who only stand and jeer:
Talking Dirty   49
I wanted to write a talking-dirty sonnet,
Match.com.sonnet   50
We're too well matched and not at all, these guys.

MARILYN L. TAYLOR:
The Seven Very Liberal Arts: A Crown Of Sonnets
1. Logic   51
A moment's peace from you, old Earth—enough's
2. Grammar   52
My dear Professor, write a book on me—
3. Music   53
If I can promise you a frosty draft
4. Rhetoric   54
Shut up. Shut up, shut up, shut up. Okay?
5. Geology   55
Hold it!—hold everything—I'm falling off
6. Arithmetic   56
Mmm-mm, it melts the very core of me
7. Astronomy   57
Frédéric Chopin, Fannie Mendelssohn,

MARILYN HACKER
Future Conditional   58
After the supper dishes, let us start
Symbiose II   59
We never begin drinking before seven.
from Scars on Paper   60
Aglow in summer evening, a desk-lamp's yellow

Michael Salcman
The Sulfurous Days Of Summer   61
How often I have lain on a green haze

Molly Peacock
Couple Sharing A Peach   62
It's not the first time
Have You Ever Faked An Orgasm?   63
When you get nervous, it's so hard not to.
I Consider The Possibility   64
Long-waisted, tender-skinned and, despite the gym,

David Lehman
Split   65
Here's to the duality of flesh
To Summer   66
Shall I compare a season to a day,

Leslie Monsour
At the Summer Poetry Festival   67
Ah there she is, all siren-like and fair,

David Bergman
In Nordstrom's   68
Anything could be written on this face—

Kate Bernadette Benedict
Celibate Observances   69
Untouched, untouching: yet am I not caressed?

Maryann Corbett
Rose Catalogue in January   70
You want them, yes, the year's new hybrid teas,

TIM DLUGOS
Spy Of Love   71
New numbers in your address book (I looked).
Sonnet   72
I didn't want to tell you that I kept

DAVID W. LANDRUM
From the Chinese of Huang O (c. 400 AD)   73
You held my lotus blossom in your hand

JULIE KANE
Finale   74
How you'd begin would never be the same;

TERRI WITEK
Edith Sitwell and the Carnal World
1.   75
Viewer, it's night. I'm locked into a straightening device.
2.   76
That year I got "The Rape of the Lock" by heart

DAVID TRINIDAD
At the Glass Onion, 1971   77
He stood behind me while I played pinball

SUSAN MCLEAN
Dark Shadows   78
A high-school friend was hooked on the mystique
Your Other Women   79
Your secretaries, eager to assist you;

KIM ADDONIZIO
First Poem For You   80
I love to touch your tattoos in complete
Stolen Moments   81
What happened, happened once. So now it's best
So What   82
Guess what. If love is only chemistry—

MEREDITH BERGMANN
The Daemon Lover   83
I've been unfaithful to you with my wife,
Flash and Spark   84
My husband feels too hot, his heart a furnace

MARY MERIAM
Melon Balls   85
What do I know of sex in my seclusion,

SHARON DOLIN
Wanting Two: A Sonnet/Ghazal   86
Is the lightning zip, knotty rough
Now That I have Lain with You   87
Now that I have lain with you

ROBERT CRAWFORD
French Braids   88
While one hand is content to touch, admire
Kitchen Remodeling   89
I know I should be listening to your

DAVID ROTHMAN
She Receives Flowers   90
"Late in life you don't expect romance.

Volcano of Blossoms   91
Jungle everywhere. The cries of birds.

H.L. H<small>IX</small>
I Will Start by Telling You an Ancient Legend   92
She smiled when she passed him. He started when
As Though the Weather Were Bad in the World of Sexuality   93
The man with the crooked dick shines his shoes.
This Morally Neutralized Domain of Intercourse   94
The man with the crooked dick strikes a match.

W<small>ENDY</small> V<small>IDELOCK</small>
Prufrock Takes a Formal Lover   95
Criss cross, the letters pass, the envelopes

T<small>ONY</small> B<small>ARNSTONE</small>
The Empress   96
Her breasts are blonde. Her legs are filaments
India Rubber Man at the Temple of Sin Adult Novelty Store   97
She's just a bag of skin puffed full of air
In Which He Smells Her on His Fingers   98
This is the scent persisting on my fingers.

M<small>OIRA</small> E<small>GAN</small>
Millay Goes Down   99
What lips my lips have kissed, and where, and why?
With a Line from Millay   100
What lips my lips have kissed, and where, and why?
Variation And Quick Change   101
The wily married ladies know the trick

Kathrine Varnes
The Fleshpot Sonnets, a Crown
This moment's peach—sometimes it's just enough 102
While writing towards a bivalved, cleft-fleshed fruit, 103
Will female freedom always signal fleshpot 104
I drew the blinds and said to myself, Alone, 105
A hint of death winked back behind the gingham; 106
New hymnals of sense, shaped by this bright spirit 107
I gave up padded bras, certain offence. 108

Amy Lemmon
Asymptotic 109
Love, tempered by time, pulls to strangle
Invitation 110
Loosen your tie, dear sir, admit instead

Jo Ann Clark
Scheherazade to the King, 10th Anniversary 111
Much will have changed since your last visit.

Tatyana Mishel
Slut Sonnet III 112
We smell, I burn, your knees are at my feet.
Slut Sonnet IV 113
So, Moms: Don't fade to strangers. Ripe inside

Rose Kelleher
Hiding 114
It's loud enough to make the rafters ring,
Rope 115
Rope burns. It rubs against whatever's tender—

Rafael Campo
III. Superman Is Dead   116
I used to think that immortality
IX. Your Voice   117
Last night, when we made love, I saw inside

Midge Goldberg
Flume Ride   118
Your arms slide around my waist, and we are going,
Temptress   119
Apples? No good. If I were going to try

Christopher Bakken
A Concert of Ancient Music, Houston   120
Those who think only of weakness and pain,

Laura Maffei
The Gambit   121
Your finger in my ponytail, my dear,

Lesley Wheeler
Two Swimmers   122
So sure I was you'd want to have me back

Julie Stoner
Dear John (Drafts 1-4)   123
~~Dear Bluebeard—Yes, this means I found your cache~~

A.E. Stallings
Fire Safety Drill   124
It ought to be easy to learn:
The Married Muse   125
Maybe it's too intimate for lovers:

JENNY FACTOR
Learning Stick
1. With Him   126
Eyeing a dashboard high as the San Gabriels,
2. With Her   127
Humidity lifts us tense and intricate,
3. With Me   128
Into a rhythm ruled by kgrrr and bprrrr,

ELIZABETH M. JOHNSON
from Open House (a crown)
My Focus   129
My focus is replacing you. Most times,
The Bathroom   130
The bathroom's ready for romance. It's lit

JILL ALEXANDER ESSBAUM
We Lie Like Poems   131
We lie like poems, undulating rhyme.
Oh We Are Dancing   132
Oh we are dancing. Oh we undress. Oh
I Swanned   133
I swanned at the gold calf's hoof, I whored

RANDALL MANN
The Church Militant   134
My mouth trembling was a sign of something bad.
Uncle   135
Oh, these old weeds? The heels are come hither,

CAROL QUINN
After Tsvetaeva and Mandelstam at the Kremlin Cathedral   136
Each dome supports another. One leans against

QUINCY R. LEHR
We All Have Our Needs   *137*
I watch two twentysomethings on the train

JESSICA PIAZZA
Ankylophobia: Fear of immobility of a joint   *138*
Locked here, I'm loch-jawed: a Nessie of
Apodysophilia: Love of undressing   *139*
When many veils are pared to one what more

SANDRA BEASLEY
from Chronic Medea
VII. Husband. Wife.   *140*
In here I own the voyage of your hip,

MELA KIRKPATRICK
Gaea   *141*
He scooped unhurried fingers through her hair

CHLOE HARALAMBOUS
Circe's Loom   *142*
At midnight, Circe's man blacks out, her fix

CONTRIBUTORS   *145*

ACKNOWLEDGMENTS   *157*

Hot Sonnets

Introduction

On Hot Sonnets

If the mixed-metaphor police are lurking, I'm about to get busted. In thinking, these past months, about sex and the sonnet, why they seem to be two great tastes that taste great together, I was reminded on the one hand of what Kafka said about literature, that "a book must be the axe for the frozen sea inside of us," and, on the other, of what Adrienne Rich said about her early work in form, that form was "part of the strategy—like asbestos gloves it allowed [her] to handle materials [she] couldn't pick up bare-handed." Between the bittercold glaciers of our psyches and the hot, pressurized magma of our hearts—the mixed-metaphor cops are about to cuff me, *Officer, please, give me a minute here!*—we could just have another Eyjafjallajökull on our hands.

But no. Within and because of the graceful confines of the sonnet, it's not going to blow. At least, not in a bad way.

I love sonnets. I love reading them, writing them, teaching them. It almost seems to me that, more than any other form of poetry, sonnets embody Yeats's comment about how a good poem closes with that gratifying click of fitting the lid onto a well-made box. Whether it's a swervy, curvy Italian sonnet with its few rhymes looping up, back, and around, or a solid Shakespearean argument bearing down ineluctably to its neat, closing couplet, it makes me infinitely happy to go along for that short, sweet, 14-line ride: the satisfied little gasp at a strong volta, the purr-like whirring of what stays with me after I'm done.

Sounds like I'm talking about something else, doesn't it? I am.

Iamb. I am reminded of a student who, having done a presentation on a couple of my "naughty sonnets," relayed to me how her classmates had noticed that "the music and rhythm of [my] poem acted as a stand-in for the rhythm during sex." Smart kids, those.

Iamb. I am reminded of how consensual participants understand that a large part of the fun is in the specificity of the constraint. The containment of the safeword, the safety of ritual: ABAB CDCD EFEF GG. Therein, everything can be dared. Or ABBAABBA CDECDE. The strict carapace of the sonnet, I am convinced, both allows for and engenders various human truths that are difficult: difficult to utter, sometimes difficult to read.

And to make matters even more interesting, this is the tradition that, for centuries, embodied the all-too-human, virtually-always-male, debased speaker attempting to say to his unattainable, beautiful, bordering-on-inhuman object of desire: I love you, I want you, I adore you. Not necessarily in that order, of course.

Granted, Shakespeare put us well onto the path of defying these idealizing traditions: "When my love swears that she is made of truth," indeed. And what fun it is for Modern (and contemporary) sonneteers to take the centuries-long trope and really turn it on its ear. Edna St. Vincent Millay was expert at taking the libidinous mess that lurks in most of us and putting that "chaos into fourteen lines." She admits that she too, like a cat in heat, has howled beneath the moon of "almighty Sex." She tells us freely how the "propinquity" of a man's body has led her own "stout blood" to rebel against her brain, and in a couplet that borders on the macho, concludes that the consummation of that lust won't be cause enough to talk to the guy, should they meet again. I have to admit, I admire that macho stance. Let's call it macha.

Let's imagine Beatrice jumping down from the marble pedestal, cracking her whip; Laura turning around and saying, "Francesco, please please please stop talking to me like that." Or an honest and unfettered (in this case, I mean the word figuratively) 21st century poetess who puts her hand on her hip and tells the man sitting at the bar beside her, "I want to fall in love, but not forever."

I have been that poetess. I hope, Gentle Reader, that you don't bristle at my use of that word, but I live in a land in which I hear it all the time, have even grown quite used to it: *Lei è una poetessa*. In fact, let's be honest: I've grown fond of it, that extra, sexy, sibilant set of syllables at the end. And remember that nouns are gendered here not politically, but grammatically.

You hold in your warm hands a collection of exquisite sonnets (keeping in mind that *squisito* is the word in Italian for delicious) that explore the joys of the one-night stand and of married love; the soft, the sweet, the warm embrace, and the crack of leather onto bare flesh; the gay, the straight, the celibate; taste, smell, (obviously) touch, and sound, and the visual, the "bivalve, cleft-fleshed fruit," "that wiggly bulbous member."

In compiling this anthology, we strove to find sonnets that would appeal to a broad audience of poetry lovers. We made the decisions (and they were hard to make) not to include sonnets in translation, nor authors previous to the great sonnet-mistress Edna St. Vincent Millay. Obviously, many Hot Sonnets were written before the 20th century, but one argument of this book is that rumors of the death of the sonnet have been greatly exaggerated. Between these covers you will find sexy, contemporary sonnets that are philosophical, funny, mordant, romantic, dangerous, thought-provoking, and/or simply, delightfully naughty.

Moira Egan

An editor's note

My Dear Old Sonnet

MY DEAR OLD SONNET, mother of my muse,
how can so small a creature hold such power?
You nag me: "Tidy up! Waste not! It's now or
never, just get it done! So what's to lose?
A dozen lines plus two, some rhymes, in booze-
talk that amounts to half a pint. An hour
or less. Try singing an octave in the shower!
(Of course, be careful of the words you choose.)"

And yet I know this sawed-off biddy loves me.
Loves me as much when I'm running hot and wild
and wicked as when my breathing's measured, mild.
She doesn't look askance when I talk dirty
and loves the men who say they like it. She
knows without routine I can't be free.

                          Clarinda Harriss

Edna St. Vincent Millay

CXXV

I TOO BENEATH YOUR MOON, almighty Sex,
Go forth at nightfall crying like a cat,
Leaving the lofty tower I laboured at
For birds to foul and boys and girls to vex
With tittering chalk; and you, and the long necks
Of neighbors sitting where their mothers sat
Are well aware of shadowy this and that
In me, that's neither noble nor complex.
Such as I am, however, I have brought
To what it is, this tower; it is my own;
Though it was reared To Beauty, it was wrought
From what I had to build with: honest bone
Is there, and anguish; pride; and burning thought;
And lust is there, and nights not spent alone.

Edna St. Vincent Millay

xli

I, BEING BORN A WOMAN and distressed
By all the needs and notions of my kind,
Am urged by your propinquity to find
Your person fair, and feel a certain zest
To bear your body's weight upon my breast:
So subtly is the fume of life designed,
To clarify the pulse and cloud the mind,
And leave me once again undone, possessed.
Think not for this, however, the poor treason
Of my stout blood against my staggering brain,
I shall remember you with love, or season
My scorn with pity,—let me make it plain:
I find this frenzy insufficient reason
For conversation when we meet again.

Edna St. Vincent Millay

xcvii

WHEN WE ARE OLD and these rejoicing veins
Are frosty channels to a muted stream,
And out of all our burning there remains
No feeblest spark to fire us, even in dream,
This be our solace: that it was not said
When we were young and warm and in our prime,
Upon our couch we lay as lie the dead,
Sleeping away the unreturning time.
O sweet, O heavy-lidded, O my love,
When morning strikes her spear upon the land,
And we must rise and arm us and reprove
The insolent daylight with a steady hand,
Be not discountenanced if the knowing know
We rose from rapture but an hour ago.

e.e. cummings

xxiv.

and this day it was Spring...us
drew lewdly the murmurous minute clumsy
smelloftheworld. We intricately
alive,cleaving the luminous stammer of bodies
(eagerly just not each other touch)seeking,some
street which easily tickles a brittle fuss
of fragile huge humanity...
       Numb
thoughts,kicking in the rivers of our blood,miss
by how terrible inches speech—it
made you a little dizzy did the world's smell
(but i was thinking why the girl-and-bird
of you move...moves...and also,i'll admit—)

till,at the corner of Nothing and Something,we heard
a handorgan in twilight playing like hell

e.e. cummings

ii.

when I have thought of you somewhat too
much and am become perfectly and
simply Lustful…sense a gradual stir
of beginning muscle,and what it will do
to me before shutting…understand
i love you…feel your suddenly body reach
for me with a speed of white speech

(the simple instant of perfect hunger
Yes)
    how beautifully swims
the fooling world in my huge blood,
cracking brains A swiftlyenormous light
—and furiously puzzling through,prismatic,whims,
the chattering self perceives with hysterical fright

a comic tadpole wriggling in delicious mud

e.e. cummings

vii.

AFTER YOUR POPPIED HAIR inaugurates
Twilight, with earnest of what pleading pearls;
After the carnal vine your beauty curls
Upon me, with such tingling opiates
As immobile my literal flesh awaits;
Ere the attent wind spiritual whirls
Upward the murdered throstles and the merles
Of that prompt forest which your smile creates;

Pausing, I lift my eyes as best I can,
Where twain frail candles close their single arc
Upon a water-colour by Cézanne.
But you, love thirsty, breathe across the gleam;
For total terror of the actual dark
Changing the shy equivalents of dream.

John Berryman

Sonnet #1

I WISHED ALL THE MILD DAYS of middle March
This special year, your blond good-nature might
(Lady) admit—kicking abruptly tight
With will and affection down your breast like starch—
Me to your story, in Spring, and stretch, and arch.
But who not flanks the wells of uncanny light
Sudden in bright sand towering? A bone sunned white.
Considering travellers bypass these and parch.

This came to less yes than an ice cream cone
Let stand...though still my sense of it is brisk:
Blond silky cream, sweet cold, aches: a door shut.
Errors of order! Luck lies with the bone,
Who rushed (and rests) to meet your small mouth, risk
Your teeth irregular and passionate.

John Berryman

Sonnet #4

AH WHEN YOU DRIFT hover before you kiss
More my mouth yours now, lips grow more to mine
Teeth click, suddenly your tongue like a mulled wine
Slides fire,—I wonder what the point of life is.
Do, down this night where I adore you, Lise,
So I forsake the blest assistant shine
Of deep-laid maps I made for summits, swine-
enchanted lover, loafing in the abyss?

Loaf hardly, while my nerves dance, while the gale
Moans like your hair down here. But I lie still,
Strengthless and smiling under a maenad rule.
Whose limbs worked once, whose imagination's grail
Many or some would nourish, must now I fill
My strength with desire, my cup with your tongue,
   no more Melpomene's, but Erato's fool?...

Hayden Carruth

Sonnet 9

TO SEE A WOMAN long oppressed by fear
come free at last is joyous and a wonder.
As a poet I don't care for the stale remainder
of conventional sonnetry, yet just to savor
my own outpouring pleasure in this affair
I must lean backward lazily, as it were,
in the old romantic bed, an absconder
and apostate in my era. Today I wonder
where love's ideas lead me, and I don't care.

Well, she is like a *flower*. Let's say a Turk's cap
      lily. Somehow the nodding horn has lifted
and its complex hazel smile has opened
to the light. More, more, it has *wafted*
a clear high tone like a trumpet from the steppe
of home to heaven, that there has never happened.

Willis Barnstone

With a French Nun in Lapland

EVEN THE CONSTANT SUN wears a small coat
of darkness till it bangs into our light.
A nun in Lapland on a ferry boat,
whose lips are frozen God, whose hood is white
with ice floating the fjords, unzips my pants
to show her grace. "I'll keep this memory,"
she whispers, "in my bones and sardine cans
back in the factory where I share my tea
and labor with the workers." Sun hangs on
all night in Lapland in July. I bless
my friend the nun for sun. A socialist
and French she talked to clouds over our fun
and deer licks. When our bellies join, no less
than mountains blush and crush us in their fist.

Thom Gunn

Diagrams

DOWNTOWN, AN OFFICE TOWER is going up.
And from the mesa of unfinished top
Big cranes jut, spectral points of stiffened net:
Angled top-heavy artefacts, and yet
Diagrams from the sky, as if its air
Could drop lines, snip them off, and leave them there.

On girders round them, Indians pad like cats,
With wrenches in their pockets and hard hats.

They wear their yellow boots like moccasins,
Balanced where air ends and where steel begins,
Sky men, and through the sole's flesh, chewed and pliant,
They feel the studded bone-edge of the giant.
It grunts and sways through its whole metal length.
And giving to the air is sign of strength.

Grace Cavalieri

Anna Nicole's Dream

A CUP OF JEWELS, a star, flying dragons,
Rainbows, a bright diamond crown,
Baby octopus, pirate ships, golden dragoons,
Fairy dust, clouds, snow mist on the ground,
Enchanted woods, Cherry trees, a crystal room,
Conifers and Pines, Magnolias in season,
Tea cups made of acorns where toadstools bloom,
White bunnies, green elves, Azalea breezes,
A picture book with her photo in light,
Love's handprint on the cement of her heart,
Russian soldiers protecting her stables at night,
Three bluebirds, twin cardinals, a morning skylark.
But who are these men blocking light in her room?
Without sun, how can Anna's fake tulips bloom?

Wesli Court

Sports Harassment Embarrassment 2010
> *After losing to Baltimore the Jets lose again:*
> *A Courtwright sonnet*

THE DAY WHEN INEZ SAINZ came marching in
To tackle the Jets' steamy locker room
And get an interview on her recorder
She billed herself "the hottest sports reporter
In Mexico." The players were abloom,
Sweaty and florid, showing a lot of skin.
She tried hard not to notice they had shed
Their shorts and towels—at least that's what she said.

But it was hard to miss each whistle, call,
And all the balls the coaches threw to land
Not far from where she stood. Then quarterback
Mark Sanchez arrived; he took up the slack
And handled her like a pro. She played the hand
She had been dealt, but swore she'd never crawl.

Wesli Court

Venal Song

HOUR ON HOUR I'VE WANDERED Venus' arbor
Looking for the sun. All I encounter
Are dappled leaves and lichen. In her bower
She stands disarmed. Each time I try to mount her

I fall unmembered to the harlot moss,
The victim of her concrete passion, dazzled
And confused. I try to fit my loss
Into her cross words, but my mind is puzzled—

Incomplete and wretched intellect
Is hardly help at all. Before the tomb
Of love I stand and pray to be elect,
To be at one with her in her blue womb,

For there at least and last I could not fault her,
And I'd have no more reason to assault her.

Michael Cantor

The Love of Sushi Sue
#1

I LIVED NEAR TOKYO'S Hama-Zushi bar
those years I was a seafood sybarite—
would start off there with monkfish caviar
and sweet live shrimp, to set the appetite—
then grab a cab to narrow streets where night
rolled into dawn, and hunt for something more.
I'd often wander home about first light
to find Old Hama, sweeping out the store.
He'd eye the catch that wriggled past his door,
but knew my true love was an artful blow-
fish broth, or chunks of fatty tuna, raw,
caressed with strands of gleaming herring roe.
Good food was all I worshipped and revered
and women, though amusing, interfered.

Michael Cantor

#2

IN TIME, THE REAL-LIFE girlfriends disappeared,
replaced by fantasies of Sushi Sue
who, naked as a salmon, commandeered
my reveries—slim sushi ingenue
enshrined behind Old Hama's bleached bamboo.
She worked like nude quicksilver, with a blade
in each small hand—Hama's fish swam through
her fingers and in seconds were fileted,
embraced by rice and seaweed, and arrayed
with fat carp's heads and pouting silver bream—
sea urchin eggs, fresh squid and trout—displayed
as backdrop for my slick, wet ocean dream.
But Sue repelled me when I cupped her breast:
"A sushi girl cannot make love to guest!"

Michael Cantor

#3

ALTHOUGH ALL THAT WAS years ago, the quest
remains. My thoughts have never wandered far
from Hama's pickled prawns with lemon zest,
the earthy taste of slow-baked arctic char—
or Sushi Sue's small room behind the bar—
where I now nibble her *hirame*, coax
the sweetness from her *uni*, feel a star
ignite within me as she lightly strokes
my *ana-kyu*, and whispers private jokes.
At last, with sake nips and salty sips,
I polish off a banquet that evokes
a sigh—and *mirugai*—from parted lips.
"I'm glad that you like raw fish," she will coo,
as I finally taste the love of Sushi Sue.

Glossary
  hirame: Halibut. Often served as a sashimi-style first course, with a *ponzu* dipping sauce (lime juice, soy sauce and sake). Good *hirame* should be so fresh and sliced so thinly that you can see through it, and detect the pattern on a plate; and it is supposedly ordered as a first course to enable a foodie to quickly evaluate the sushi shop.
  uni: Sea urchin gonads.
  ana-kyu: A conical, hand-made sushi specialty of rice, cucumber strips and ocean eel, rolled in seaweed and topped with a thick, sweet sauce. This is much more elegant than the tight "California roll" style popular in the States, and superb *ana-kyu* is regarded as one of the criteria of a fine, traditional sushi establishment. (Warning—it's impossible to eat the thing without having the dark brown sauce drip through the bottom of the cone and down your arm. *Ana-kyu* devotees are distinguished by stains of honor on their wrists and forearms, not unlike the nicotine-drenched fingers of post-war French intellectuals.)
  mirugai: A large clam. Analogous to a New England quahog.

Clarinda Harriss

Thunder

THEY ALSO SERVE who only stand and jeer:
that seemed to be the theory of the boys haunting
Mom's Diesel Stop and Convenience Store
on Route 50 in '52. So what if we were flaunting
whatever budding bumps and nubbins jabbed
though our size-S shirts. It was a lightning
revelation, how our mere passing hocked up gobs
of spit from deep in their gut till strings
of mumbles dripped from the corners of their mouths.
How many years before it would dawn
on us that people actually did, for love,
what the truckstop jockeys claimed
they had in mind for us, I wonder—
or what real tenderness drowned in diesel thunder.

Clarinda Harriss

Talking Dirty

I WANTED TO WRITE a talking-dirty sonnet,
most probably Petrarchan—dirty words
rhyme well, though dentally (a bit absurd—
they should be labial.) I'd get right on it
except that limericks have been there, done it,
and those hard sounds might cramp the sweet first third
of sex's poem, the slow swell, the blurred
divide between perhaps and have-to-have it.

And yet—what romance lacks a volta, vital
or fatal? Love's halves, asymmetrical
always, maintain a shaky poise; in time,
may teeter toward a murderous punch-line.
The poem writes itself. We lie in trance,
but *love, fuck, trouble* hum their assonance.

Clarinda Harriss

Match.com.sonnet

WE'RE TOO WELL MATCHED and not at all, these guys.
Love is not love nor even like, not when
the itch of them is like the itch of jeans
too tight in the crotch, too low in the so-called rise.
It's true I like the color of their eyes,
but like mine more, although we wear the same
gray-brown-green-yellow-nothing which we name
(for no reason known to me) "hazel." We're wise

to wend some other way of thinking. Are
my tits real? That's a good one, so endearing.
Say, do you stuff your cod piece? No use asking
now, I have my answer, and apparently you aren't
about to take my own for truth. No matter, hon.
About Viagra—look, it's half past one.

Marilyn L. Taylor

The Seven Very Liberal Arts: A Crown Of Sonnets

According to Plato and Aristotle, the liberal arts are the subjects suitable for the development of intellectual and moral excellence, as distinguished from those that are merely useful and practical.

1. Logic

A MOMENT'S PEACE from you, old Earth—enough's
enough! Your gorgeousness is still in season,
still clobbering philosophy and reason
in one delicious blow. Show me your stuff,
and dump "The Liberal Arts", that old flim-flammery
that goes like this (my drop-dead parlor-trick):
Logic, Grammar, Music, Rhetoric,
Geology, Arithmetic, Astronomy.

They're very easy to recite, but hard
as hell to live with. Ever try to dance
with Logic, to unzip its crotchety pants,
get sexy deconstructing Kierkegaard?
Unpromising. Like bathing with a cat.
And no one needs to write a book on that.

Marilyn L. Taylor

2. Grammar

My dear Professor, write a book on me—
devote a chapter to my graceful lines,
and how my every syllable defines
the dips and rises of my prosody.
Come scan me carefully—and when you're through
deal with my feet, iambic and trochaic,
pronounce them perfect (if a touch archaic);
then taste the syllables in my haiku.

Scribble suggestions slowly down my spine
with your intense, exploratory care,
and punctuate, with sharp intakes of air
the way my staves and strophes intertwine.
And then, Professor, sign me fore and aft,
as if I were a promising first draft.

Marilyn L. Taylor

3. Music

If I can promise you a frosty draft
of Bud Lite when we get there, can we go
to Nashville? Kansas City? Branson Mo?
I'm craving country music—that whole raft
of anthems from the boys who do it best,
star-twangled-banners from the girls who strayed
and lied and loved, and finally got laid
by some hot cowpoke in a leather vest.

Been thinking, off and on, of Toby Keith,
the way his fingers pluck that blue guitar;
I dream up porno movies (he's the star)
on how those fingers feel from underneath—
but never mind; it's high time we departed.
Get in the car. Shut up. Don't get me started.

Marilyn L. Taylor

4. Rhetoric

SHUT UP. Shut up, shut up, shut up. Okay?
You're not my lucky star, you are a damn
black hole. I do not love you, Sam-I-am.
Get lost. Scram. Beat it. Go away.
Clear out your retrosexual groceries—
that loaf of bread, the jug of wine—right now;
and as for your adoring little *thou*,
just watch her kick you in the fantasies.

I get the sense you're painfully aware
that you're a sorry-ass. The Big Dumpee.
How sad. Let me extend my sympathy
by offering you a simple little prayer:
May your next cocktail be a Molotov,
and everything that you hold dear fall off.

Marilyn L. Taylor

5. Geology

Hold it!—hold everything—I'm falling off
the edge (there goes my equilibrium—
so long!) because of you and your sublime
topography. You're dangerous enough
to cause a tremor, a gigantic lurch,
a nine on my internal Richter scale.
You pulse with something seismically male
and I'm no safer on my little perch
than in a shack along the San Andreas.
How can I ever rise above the rubble
of what you've done to me—stay out of trouble
when aftershocks will certainly betray us?
A tougher question than I bargained for;
remember, I am molten at the core.

Marilyn L. Taylor

6. Arithmetic

Mmm-mm, it melts the very core of me
to listen to the cheerful clink and jingle
in your deep pockets. I begin to tingle
when you declare that I'm your chickadee,
and you're my guaranteed annuity,
my piggy bank, my Google IPO;
and should you strike out in a year or so,
I could become your 501(c)3.

A little bit of Warren Buffetry
is all it took—a little real estate,
a tiny merger—to emancipate
those lovely megabucks. I do agree
the time has clearly come for you to lay
your Freddie Mac against my Fannie Mae.

Marilyn L. Taylor

7. Astronomy

Frédéric Chopin, Fannie Mendelssohn,
Claude Debussy—when you woke up at night
(synapses snapping wildly) did you write
your nocturnes then? And was the woozy moon
spreading its silver fingers over yours,
convincing you to give in to your will,
your High Romantic fantasies, until
the swollen stars were winking like voyeurs?

How intimate were you with the coiled wires
underneath the piano's lid—as note
by note you wove a lovely antidote
for our enormous, orbiting desires?
Did you suspect how much it would be worth
to bring one moment's peace to this old earth?

Marilyn Hacker

Future Conditional

AFTER THE SUPPER DISHES, let us start
where we left off, my knees between your knees,
half in the window seat. O let me, please,
hands in your hair, drink in your mouth. Sweetheart,
your body is a text I need the art
to be constructed by. I halfway kneel
to your lap, propped by your thighs, and feel
burning my hand, your privacy, your part
armor underwear. This time I'll loose
each button from its hole; I'll find the hook,
release promised abundance to this want,
while your hands, please, here and here, exigent
and certain, open this; it is, this book,
made for your hands to read, your mouth to use.

Marilyn Hacker

Symbiose II

WE NEVER BEGIN DRINKING before seven.
We almost always have good appetites.
We always have good sex on Tuesday nights.
We like to give as good as we are given.
We like to do it in the morning; do
it also evenings between six and eight-
thirty. We like to have our dinner late.
We try to keep the body count to two
dead soldiers: this with moderate success.
We do get headaches, but we don't get cramps.
We take less than a half an hour to dress;
need: pockets, details, stuffs that please the touch.
We do it once like ladies, once like tramps.
We love each other very very much.

Marilyn Hacker

from Scars on Paper

AGLOW IN SUMMER EVENING, a desk-lamp's yellow
moonlight peruses notebooks, houseplants, texts,
while an ageing woman thinks of sex
in the present tense. Desire may follow,
urgent or elegant, cut raw or mellow
with wine and ripe black figs: a proof, the next
course, a simple question, the complex
response, a burning sweetness she will swallow.
The opening mind is sexual and ready
to embrace, incarnate in its prime.
Rippling concentrically from summer's gold
disc, desire's iris expands, steady
with blood-beat. Each time implies the next time.
The ageing woman hopes she will grow old.

Michael Salcman

The Sulfurous Days Of Summer

How often I have lain on a green haze
of lawn, soaking up the sulfurous days
of summer. How often I have thought my life
reborn when, pinked and over-ripe,
I've spied a pair of breasts
levitating before my eyes, like two crests
on a wave poised to come ashore,
its shadow fantastic on the ocean floor,
smashing razor clams and oyster shells
into uncountable grains, pounding in the swells.
But the image ebbs away like love's fingers in the dark
or any imagined glory as wide off the mark
from the real as thinking is from feeling,
or this vain hope, as death is from non-being.

Molly Peacock

Couple Sharing A Peach

It's not the first time
we've bitten into a peach.
But now at the same time
it splits—half for each.
Our "then" is inside its "now,"
its halved pit unfleshed—

what was refreshed.
Two happinesses unfold
from one joy, folioed.
In a hotel room
our moment lies
with its ode inside,
a red tinge,
with a hinge.

Molly Peacock

Have You Ever Faked an Orgasm?

WHEN YOU GET NERVOUS, it's so hard not to.
When you're expected to come in something
other than your ordinary way, to
take pleasure in the new way, lost, not knowing

how to drive it back to sureness...*where are
the thousand thousand flowers I always pass,
the violet flannel, then the sharpness?*
You can't, you can't...extinguish the star

in a burst. It goes on glowing. That head
between your legs so long. Could it really
want to be there? One whimpers as though...
then gets mad. One could smash the other's valiant head.

"You didn't come, did you?" Naturally, he knows.
Although I try to lie, the truth escapes me
almost like an orgasm itself. Then the "No"
that should crack a world, but doesn't, slips free.

Molly Peacock

I Consider the Possibility

LONG-WAISTED, TENDER-SKINNED and, despite the gym,
love roll about the midriff above the leggy limbs
muscled into knots at each calf, "beautiful for your age"
— bend over naked from your waist and show your red half-
peach of cunt to me who has fumbled at my cage
trying key after key in the stuck door with a half-laugh
after each failure; let me lay the bone of my nose
on the peach flesh and lift up my mouth to the pit
as I reach my arms toward the inverted throes
of your breasts, and as I touch your orange nipple tips
know that all my life I've wanted only men
and now, dispossessed of my neglectful mother
who herself toyed with the choice of women,
and upon being merrily teased by my therapist
at the prospect of such a love affair (the male "other"
has never incited such laughter), let me touch your wrist
at the dinner table and begin the silly maneuver
that will lead me to hold your head, to smooth your
hair all back, as in going through keys at the door my wrist
finally turns tender side up as the lock untwists.

David Lehman

Split

HERE'S TO THE DUALITY of flesh
and blood, neck and rope,
and the temporary flush
of skin, absence of hope.

Here's to his length and her depth.
As far as foreplay is indicted,
the whole vice squad is invited:
gambling, booze, dope, and death.

Here's to her autumn and his fall.
If fucking is the athleticism of the saints,
he will paint her not as a painter paints
a woman but as a painter paints a wall.

You will become addicted to his smell,
so use it well or not at all.

David Lehman

To Summer

SHALL I COMPARE A SEASON to a day,
a woman to a body like a violin?
Summer is the reason for my grin,
and on that violin I would play.

In the nave of her church I would pray.
Though summer's lease hath all too short a date,
I shall fall into winter and spring to my fate,
and while you wait I'll be frank and sing "My Way."

But just as a whole is greater than the sum
of its parts, or 'twere a bummer, rank indeed,
so a garden outlives its fiercest weed
to blossom under my green thumb.
On her I shall gaze from head to bum.
Where Summer follows I shall lead.

Leslie Monsour

At the Summer Poetry Festival
after Dick Davis's "At the Reception"

AH THERE SHE IS, all siren-like and fair,
The one who needs a boost with her career.
She has a manuscript she's peddling.
I've heard it's so-so, but I'll praise the thing.
My Pulitzer and sultry, southern lilt
Routinely do the trick; she'll all but wilt
Into my arms. I see she wears a ring.
So much the easier to have a fling.

She's caught my stare. I'll raise my glass and wink.
What luck, she has my book and wants a drink,
And I am right between her and the bar.
Sign it for you? With pleasure, yes, my dear.
No pen? No matter. Later on we'll go
And look for one inside my bungalow.

David Bergman

In Nordstrom's

ANYTHING COULD BE written on this face—
he is that young and unmarked
by imperfection, the skin smooth, the green
eyes grass at dawn. He finds my toes
in the shoes that are too long. He brings
out a size smaller. "Walk on them," he says.
"How do they feel?" he asks. In the presence
of such beauty, one forgets one's age and then
grows painfully aware of it. "They look good
on you," he nods, smiling. And for the first time
I notice all his clothes are wrong,
that any clothing would be wrong on the fine
light structure of his bones that were built
only for wings. Just wings.

Kate Bernadette Benedict

Celibate Observances

UNTOUCHED, UNTOUCHING: yet am I not caressed?
Not long ago I never would have guessed
how hotly burns the slowly dwindling flame.
I lodge inside Libido's ample frame
of soft sensation and unhurried need.
Seized by chastity, by chastity freed,
to give myself to every worthy thing,
the daily agon and the daily wandering,
as now I tingle in the leaves and roots
where autumn ginkgoes drop their musky fruits.
How rousing, to rededicate your trust,
let youth go, and reconsecrate your lust!
Rapture's steadfast, solitude is bliss.
Then why do I seek it still: a human kiss?

Maryann Corbett

Rose Catalogue in January

You want them, yes, the year's new hybrid teas,
long-stemmed, high-centered, pointed, budded tight.
You hesitate at old varieties'
neediness, at fogs of pesticide,
thorny defenses, sensitivities—

But close your eyes. Think how you loved them once,
those hundred-petalled secrecies within
Fantin-Latour, those foldings, sinuous, dense.
Think of rugosa petals' openness,
of rounded hips that bore the weight of winter,

and albas: how their breathings stir the past.
How essence, concentrated, will persist,
complexities still fragrant on the air
when nothing's left but fragments in a jar.

Tim Dlugos

Spy Of Love

NEW NUMBERS in your address book (I looked).
Let's not go, gentle, into that. Good night,
I'll call you in the morning, though you might
be sleeping now with someone else . . . I'm hooked

on jealousy and speed, high on my list
of dark emotions. Took a walk at ten
this evening where the sulfur lamps pretend
they're sunlight, though their quirky waves have missed

the vitamins we store up in our eyes.
Depletion and allowance bring me here
to Brooklyn and to poverty. It's clear
that something's got to give. Perhaps "'tis I,"

though rats alone live in my granary.
The spy of love feeds on chicanery.

Tim Dlugos

Sonnet

I DIDN'T WANT TO TELL you that I kept
What I collected when the typhoon swept
Through Pakistan in 1969.
I emptied the donation box to dine
In style with friends. The millions that I raised
For UNICEF years later never blazed
To burn away a theft I chose to hide.
For want of what I stole, how many died?

Nor did I want to share the afternoons
In grungy storefronts stalking horny goons.
Sex of a sort—dispirited, forlorn.
Damp walls, waist-level holes, and grainy porn.

Bravado masked my faithlessness and shame.
One secret left: my life's one love's real name.

David W. Landrum

From the Chinese of Huang O (c. 400 AD)

You held my lotus blossom in your hand
So gently, and you played a marvelous game,
Your lips upon the pistil. When I came,
We took some rhino horn, and my demand
For more and more received no reprimand.
You fucked me all night long! You had no shame!
All night the rooster's gorgeous crest, in flame,
Stood up, bright red. As bees in flowers stand
And gather nectar, you were lodged in me,
And trembled at my stamens, perfumed jewel.
So you shall have my all. It would be cruel
For someone else to plumb my lotus pond.
You make my blossoms fire with love so fond
And passion deeper than the eastern sea.

Julie Kane

Finale

How you'd begin would never be the same;
at times you'd even face me for a while.
But always, in that drive before you came,
you'd flip me over, finish doggy-style.
Another funny thing: you'd never try
to steal a peek at me when I undressed.
I wondered if you'd rather have a guy,
if that was why you covered up my breasts.
Or maybe I was wrong, and you were straight,
but ex or mama used to yak, yak, yak;
you'd shove my mouth into the pillowcase
to face an uncommunicative back.
I haven't met her yet, your newest friend,
and yet I'd bet my butt about the end.

Terri Witek

Edith Sitwell and the Carnal World
1.

VIEWER, IT'S NIGHT. I'm locked into a straightening device.
So remove my flesh like an overly bulky gown
and trace my spine's delicious curve, my nose's
(one nostril's been closed by a metal flap) small bend,
and the place where you can plump up like a heart
behind twin bars. I can still breathe one-sided poetry so will—
that the night, though long, retains a certain nasty gleam
can be seen in its spirits: fat bluebottle flies which have descended
(it's summer in Staffordshire), are drawn to the usual small,
dead thing, and are far more beautiful, in their blue carapaces,
than they deserve. But lost and stupid too.
What can they learn to love that's here?
You've already picked me clean, bright thing—
you know the answer, beat doubled fists, and can't refuse.

Terri Witek

Edith Sitwell and the Carnal World
2.

THAT YEAR I GOT "The Rape of the Lock" by heart
instead of "The Boy Stood on the Burning Deck"
(not that poem's right name). I learned "The Rape of the Lock"
not only because my parents deemed it so improper
but because coiled in that metonymic was my hope
that if new worlds could be sprung from a single lock
small me might be fanned to larger, warmer you.
Besides, I loved the *billet-doux*, coiffure posed
as subject, and that canny lovers might manage
to couple handily within each couplet
without quite touching. A lack turned luck indeed.
As if a girl with a book stands in for boys on decks
while something both licks the stalled-out amidships higher
and also retrieves the broom that beats it back.

David Trinidad

At the Glass Onion, 1971

HE STOOD BEHIND ME while I played pinball
in a corner of the bar. He rubbed his
hard-on against my jeans. It was the fall
after the rape. Nineteen, I was a wiz

at the game, but as he ran his large hand
along the inside of my thighs and said
how much he wanted to take me home and
fuck me, I glanced up at the flashing red

and white lights and let my last ball slide past
the flippers. Instead of getting more change,
as I'd said, I bypassed the bar and dashed
into the bathroom. No lock, though. "You're strange,"

he said, tugging. I looked down at his head
till someone knocked, stuffed my wet cock, and fled.

Susan McLean

Dark Shadows

A HIGH-SCHOOL FRIEND was hooked on the mystique
of vampires, filled with vaguely sexy dread
by Barnabas, who, if he weren't undead,
would look like a forlorn and haggard geek.
She watched his daytime soap five times a week,
voraciously. At nineteen, when she wed,
she decked her windows and the waterbed
in purple-velvet mortuary chic.

But who am I to talk? I had my own
Vlad the Impaler, singing in a band—
I, too, a good girl eager to depart
from goodness, but determined to disown
complicity, pretend I'd never planned
to say "Give me that stake right through my heart."

Susan McLean

Your Other Women

Your secretaries, eager to assist you;
your colleagues, protegées, even your dean;
the shopgirls who, you joke, cannot resist you;
my own best friends; the maid who comes to clean;
the women whom you've charmed in conversation;
the students who adore you from afar—
how can I resent their admiration,
knowing, better than they, how good you are?

So pick your favorite starlets for your spree
and rent each film they've been in from the start—
I won't complain. How can I say you're wrong
to ogle blondes you swear all look like me?
For when our jobs require long weeks apart,
we both know what it takes to get along.

Kim Addonizio

First Poem For You

I LOVE TO TOUCH your tattoos in complete
darkness, when I can't see them. I'm sure of
where they are, know by heart the neat
lines of lightning pulsing just above
your nipple, can find, as if by instinct, the blue
swirls of water on your shoulder where a serpent
twists, facing a dragon. When I pull you

to me, taking you until we're spent
and quiet on the sheets, I love to kiss
the pictures in your skin. They'll last until
you're seared to ashes; whatever persists
or turns to pain between us, they will still
be there. Such permanence is terrifying.
So I touch them in the dark; but touch them, trying.

Kim Addonizio

Stolen Moments

WHAT HAPPENED, HAPPENED once. So now it's best
in memory—an orange he sliced: the skin
unbroken, then the knife, the chilled wedge
lifted to my mouth, his mouth, the thin
membrane between us, the exquisite orange,
tongue, orange, my nakedness and his,
the way he pushed me up against the fridge—
Now I get to feel his hands again, the kiss
that didn't last, but sent some neural twin
flashing wildly through the cortex. Love's
merciless, the way it travels in
and keeps emitting light. Beside the stove
we ate an orange. And there were purple flowers
on the table. And we still had hours.

Kim Addonizio

So What

GUESS WHAT. If love is only chemistry—
phenylethylamine, that molecule
that dizzies up the brain's back room, smoky
with hot bebop—it won't be long until
a single worker's mopping up the scuffed
and littered floor, whistling tunelessly,
each endorphin cooling like a snuffed
glass candle, the air stale with memory.
So what, you say; outside, a shadow lifts
a trumpet from its case, lifts it like an ingot
and scatters a few virtuosic riffs
toward the locked-down stores. You've quit
believing that there's more, but you're still stirred
enough to stop, and wait, and listen hard.

Meredith Bergmann

The Daemon Lover

I'VE BEEN UNFAITHFUL to you with my wife,
but you have taken pleasure that was due
to me and spent it all in daily life.
There is no us: we love another two.

This heat is how renunciation feels
while burning through a marriage. You admit
me as a flame. Your wedding ring anneals,
although we never touched, or clung, or bit.

Let our imaginations be as lavish
as if we could remember the perfume
of one with whom there was no episode
of flesh or heartache. Come, my dear, and ravish
the ordinary in your lawful room,
shades drawn. The more he gets, the more I'm owed.

Meredith Bergmann

Flash and Spark

My husband feels too hot, his heart a furnace
that, pumping forth his heat with constant thunder,
unmakes our bed to wood, to stifling forest,
and bakes our bower into bone-dry tinder.

He'll catch me close when I would stand the farthest
and probe my heart with questions, ever tender,
till, lying where the thickest oaks touch foreheads
to cool our thoughts, I think of burning timber.

But I am not some dryad, acres poorer,
who cries and flees a fire she cannot master.
I'll seek in conflagration some new power
as scorched seeds swell and quicken, given moisture,
and new growth matches strength with stronger forces.
How can I quench him? Let me burn to powder.

Mary Meriam

Melon Balls

WHAT DO I KNOW of sex in my seclusion,
the big black bull outside the hot barbed wire,
the female rancher's sweat in the confusion,
for all I know, the bad bull's balls on fire?
I'm most familiar with my quiet table,
with casseroles, with roasted nuts and seeds,
with stewing beans, with salads cool and stable,
with satisfying simple daily needs.
A smooth-skinned melon? Yes, it fits my hands.
I feel the melon's soft warm weight and think
of her. A lizard nods. He understands?
I rinse the melon in the kitchen sink
and try to let my thoughts run down the drain.
The absence of her pleasure is my pain.

Sharon Dolin

Wanting Two: A Sonnet/Ghazal

Is THE LIGHTNING ZIP, knotty rough
in your crotch not enough?

Molten multiplied to the nth
till you cry out Stop! Enough.

Band pouring on past four, you
slamming into bodies—hot enough?

Is turning to your partner pillowed, finding
all you've ever lain with—copped enough?

Is woodpecker to its tree, is you knee-
to-knee, groin-to-mouth—what's enough?

Is lion-son asleep in shade, is harte-
beest not flayed to rot enough?

Head upon breast, silk within rest, wanting
to return to desk: one's a lot—enough.

Sharon Dolin

Now That I Have Lain with You

Now that I have lain with you
You know I can be claimed by you.

Your hazel eyes, the way you linger-kiss:
I long to feel the stamen of you.

My woes unraveled to piano by Ravel,
My stricken heart's suddenly unmaimed with you.

The way you lick my breasts, my toes, my nose and O:
Away, my soul's conjoined, I'm twain with you.

Your Basenji duenna romped with my Griffon muskrat.
Our dogs and kids together: That's my dream with you.

Next time I board a train or plane, give me your vow:
Soon I'll stomp/writhe flamenco Spain with you.

My pistil's moist, deep pink—your tongue's refrain
as your anthered stalk's for mine. My swain, that's you.

Robert Crawford

French Braids

WHILE ONE HAND IS CONTENT to touch, admire
A balanced, careful weave—preserve for viewing
The beauty and the boundaries of desire—
The other hand is busy at undoing.
The quiet hand counsels restraint; afraid
To wreck the composition of composure,
It's wary of destruction just for fun.
The other wants to slip between each braid,
To tease apart the strands, let run, spill over,
Release, unbind, what was so neatly done.
Your urgent kiss decides which hand is played.
A gentle pull brings argument to closure.
Surprised, my hands attempt to catch your hair:
It falls the way the rain lets go the air.

Robert Crawford

Kitchen Remodeling

I KNOW I SHOULD BE listening to your
description of the changes that you've made,
since you implied that following this tour
I'd take the test to be your kitchen aide.
I should note where you've moved the lobster pot,
but I'm distracted by your lips, your smile,
the way your hips rest up against—well, not
your hips exactly—the edge of cool white tile.
I know you're telling me about the brand
new island and the cabinet space inside,
but it's a blur. I hope you'll understand,
forgive the fact, that I've grown glassy-eyed,
and lost, imagining what I could do
on this expanse of countertop with you.

David Rothman

She Receives Flowers

"Late in life you don't expect romance.
You don't expect to be swept off your feet.
You don't expect to have another chance.
You've learned to take the bitter with the sweet.
You have reviewed each season and its cause,
The brilliant, wind-swept days, the driving rains.
You tell yourself that there are certain laws,
That now only the harvest-time remains.
So what are you supposed to do, when feral
Leopards prowl your blood beneath the moon,
And roses, invitation spangled with peril,
Appear upon your doorstep after noon?"
Sweet friend, this is your door. He sent you flowers.
Surrender to this sight, this scent, these hours.

David Rothman

Volcano of Blossoms

JUNGLE EVERYWHERE. The cries of birds.
Green canopy that hides the sky from view.
The mountain always there, like something true
But dormant, a word awaiting other words.
Alone like every other living thing,
Tangled in vines above a simmering vent
That long ago all reason assumed was spent,
It drowses like a toucan's folded wing.
But locals claim the earth still sometimes moves
The way their parents told them it once did.
And some say soon the cleft will whisper its powers
Again when the deep rift gives and giving proves
Death less than this voluptuous pyramid,
The sky awash with shuddering and flowers.

H.L. Hix

I Will Start By Telling You an Ancient Legend

SHE SMILED WHEN SHE PASSED HIM. He started when
She smiled, having passed her more often than
He wanted to remember. He smiled when
He passed her until he learned to look down.
She smiled a smile that was no expression.
She smiled when he started, just like someone
He wanted to remember. She looked down,
He remembered, like she was no one.
She was no one. She passed him. He looked down.
He wanted to remember her, but when
She passed him, smiling without expression,
He was no one. He learned to look down.
He wanted to remember. She passed. When
She smiled at him his face began to burn.

H.L. Hix

As Though the Weather Were Bad in the World of Sexuality

THE MAN WITH THE CROOKED DICK shines his shoes.
The woman with one arm takes off her brassiere.
The man straps a dildo between his knees.
The woman stands on her head on a chair.
She wants him to kneel. He wants her to scream.
He bloodies her lip as a compromise.
She wants it at work. He wants it at home.
He curses and curses. She cries and cries.
He likes to pull her hair. She likes to bite.
He always has to be last to undress.
With someone you love, at this time of night,
It's hard to distinguish kick from caress.
The clockface would be the room's only light
Did not their bodies at contact fluoresce.

H.L. Hix

This Morally Neutralized Domain of Intercourse

THE MAN WITH THE CROOKED DICK strikes a match.
The woman with one arm breaks into flame.
The man finds a bird's skull and wants to play catch.
The woman hears the skull calling her name.
He looks out the window. She looks in the door.
He crushes a spider onto the pane.
Her sun is the ceiling. His stars are the floor.
She bites her knuckles until he feels pain.
She knows his thoughts while he still has to guess.
He knows when she knows what he has to learn.
His favorite word is now. Her word is yes.
Apart, each is only radiant stone,
But one touch brings them to critical mass.
He likes to burn things and she likes to burn.

Wendy Videlock

Prufrock Takes a Formal Lover

CRISS CROSS, THE LETTERS PASS, the envelopes
each carrying an unrequited kiss.
The girl in the convertible unhooks
her jeans and idles at a four-way light

expecting lusty greens. His soda pop
is growing warm. He contemplates the time
it takes to eat a peach. The coffee shop
is rich croissants and hard-backed chairs and air

that somersaults as steam before it dares
meet lips. Years pass. She pastures her
convertible and paints the study green.
He takes his tea at noon. A bonnet blows

across the road; cross criss, the near miss—
a hundred sonnets for a sideways kiss.

Tony Barnstone

The Empress

HER BREASTS ARE BLONDE. Her legs are filaments
transmitting code that tells the cortex *flare,
illuminate the brain.* The elements
of sheen and moan and laugh are in her hair;
they mix like hormone bisque, pituitary
as lust. Her smell is dragon's blood. She slew
the dragon with her smile, a sword I carry
sheathed in my chest. Her Irish blue
is eyes and deep nights blue by candlelight
with music moving through our bodies, spasm
and tongue, and small blue thrusts, and kiss, and bite.
I love the way she gasps in blue orgasm
and grips me while my muscles clench, unwind.
Her breasts are blonde. Her mind undoes my mind.

Tony Barnstone

India Rubber Man at the Temple of Sin Adult Novelty Store

SHE'S JUST A BAG OF SKIN puffed full of air
but she's my bag of skin. I bag her in
the Red Light District, San Francisco, where
the striptease shows and bookstores sell hot sin
and vibrators and magazines and toys,
what you'd call special interest. That's when I
notice the woman browsing with the boys
who glance up from their mags to catch an eye-
ful of a real, a breathing woman. They
would like to swipe their Visa cards between
her breasts. They're desperate, I guess. Me, too. I pay
the guy, walk out and dodge a limousine
of screaming drunks, stare down a staring teen.
At home I kneel between her legs and pray.

Tony Barnstone

In Which He Smells Her on His Fingers

THIS IS THE SCENT persisting on my fingers.
This is the memory of soaping your
belly in the hot shower while your door
piled up with students. This is how it lingers
inside my pores, the smell of inside you.
This is the way I ran a nail along
the valley of your spine, took in my lungs
an inhalation of your hair—I drew
you towards me, drew a breath of you, allowed
myself to slip inside. This is the way
I kissed your eyelids, bit your lip, the day
that dawned while we were kissing on the couch,
the way you left, the way your scent remains.
This is the way I breathe you in again.

Moira Egan

Millay Goes Down

W̲ḥ̲a̲ṯ̲ ̲ḻ̲ḭ̲p̲s̲ ̲ṃ̲y̲ ̲ḻ̲ḭ̲p̲s̲ ̲ḥ̲ạ̲ṿ̲ẹ̲ ̲ḳ̲ḭ̲s̲s̲ẹ̲ḏ̲, and where, and why?
And where? Yes, there. That summer in the barn,
he'd spread me on the hay bales, sixty-nine,
oblivious to scratches, clothes half-on,
we'd take forever. Salty, sweaty both,
and kissing back the taste, each other on
each other's avid lips. I learned a truth
perhaps more grown than I was then, so when
a lady I know says she won't do this,
that that's what whores are for, it makes me sad.
It seems a gift, devotion at the source
of all our humanness; best when, instead
of needing gesture, pressure, *Please, go south*,
he softly asks me, Do you want my mouth?

Moira Egan

With a Line from Millay

W̲H̲A̲T̲ ̲L̲I̲P̲S̲ ̲M̲Y̲ ̲L̲I̲P̲S̲ ̲H̲A̲V̲E̲ ̲K̲I̲S̲S̲E̲D̲, and where, and why?
Why not's as good as why sometimes, why not
seduce this boy whose face, in candlelight,
looks slightly older, almost appropriate.
Your fingertips might almost brush his hand
as both of you dip bread into the oil.
You laugh and make it clear you understand
he'd rather hang out with a younger girl.
He says he's never had this wine, *mourvèdre*;
pronounces that he likes full-bodied, strong
and complicated wine (you think *educ-*
able, right on) and then his hand is on
your shoulder and he kisses you, his mouth
quite like a warm, *mourvèdre* fountain of youth.

Moira Egan

Variation and quick change

THE WILY MARRIED LADIES know the trick
to keeping husband happy: three parts lovin'
to one part very satisfied stomach.
(And lucky, I've had practice with the oven
as well.) But since my days of sampling guys
like flights of wine at *dégustations*
are well behind, I switch up recipes
faster than Rachael Ray. Take Sunday Chicken:
I stuff the cavity with parsley & leeks,
or fennel bulb, then rain down on it most
exotic salts: *alaea,* or, this week,
it's *fleur de sel de Guérande à la rose,*
a metaphoric, tasty melding of
what the sea gives up, and roses for my love.

Kathrine Varnes

The Fleshpot Sonnets
1.

THIS MOMENT'S PEACH—sometimes it's just enough
sweetness, despite the stone and bitter skin
or because of both, because. Because the thin
juices won't behave: soaking the white cuff
edges, filling, spilling from the palm's trough,
flesh of water, sugar gracing the chin,
tracing the neck like a contemplation of sin
we can wash away. We don't even have to bluff.

So, what will I steal tonight as the toddler sleeps?
A husband lingers in the hallway's dark
and glances, settles his eye where he'd recruit,
I with the monitor's glow upon my cheeks
two hours a day. Leave now? I can't debark
while writing towards this bivalved, cleft-fleshed fruit.

Kathrine Varnes

2.

W<small>HILE WRITING TOWARDS A BIVALVED</small>, cleft-fleshed fruit,
my left hand broke free, snaked up my sloped spine,
and unsnapped—one, two, three—(I won't refine
the moment) that strap which, unhinged, the brute
let go, at last, my girls. Of ill repute,
they flooze and dawdle, tickle and flounce, repine
over nothing firm. No wonder we confine
their laughter—unraveling the line of a tailored suit!

So goes the *brave vibrations* school of thought,
with a splash of Cixous, a touch of Carly Simon
(removing her bra in concert, famously).
Politics? License? Aesthetic liberty?
A ponderous dream of milk, *amigas*. I'm on.
Thus loosed to freedom, I become fleshpot.

Kathrine Varnes

3.

WILL FEMALE FREEDOM always signal fleshpot
to her readers? Even our girl Rosie
rivets more than we suppose, those cheeks
ripe as pomegranates. Or that sexpot
Lady Liberty herself who ought
wear more than a flimsy sheet where tourists peek
between her breezes. Oooh-la-la! Don't speak.
The minute we start to write it, are we caught?

Sometimes a woman just takes off her bra.
It's sexy as laundry in biodegradable soap.
That these illicit misses are our own
to do with as we wish (*can* one grope
one*self*?) might look like porn—if anyone saw.
I drew the blinds. I said to myself: Alone.

Kathrine Varnes

4.

I DREW THE BLINDS and said to myself, Alone,
even as I wished to see the night,
to raise the sash and bathe in pooling moonlight
while I gabbed long-distance on the phone
to voices living just outside Shoshone
where once we picnicked near the falls, a bright
July, our matriarch long since out of sight
and reach—that final skip of her thin stone.

There were peaches, wrapped in damp paper towels,
that we smoothed and lifted to our lips,
chattering aimlessly, with muddled vowels—
and one of us saw the other use her thumb
to nudge the errant prosthetic back. Such slips,
rude death peeking out from behind the gingham.

Kathrine Varnes

5.

A HINT OF DEATH winked back behind the gingham;
it was then I bit my tongue, a literal chomp
that swelled to an impediment, a lump
re-injured at the words *bosom* or *buxom*
as praise song those years that I began to blossom.
Was it ants? Or the tree roots under her rump
that prompted us up? One must be young to jump
as she did at the snap of the quilt—or well past autumn.

Four generations of women, then three, then two.
A lousy slip of the wheel, we're down to one.
So do I brood, while slicing this peach for my son,
removing the worm from the stem end, then the pit.
Whatever *peach* means to me will soon accrue
to him new sense, shaped by his own bright spirit.

Kathrine Varnes

6.

NEW HYMNALS OF SENSE, shaped by this bright spirit
calling for nuh, for nah-nah, then for nurse!
The milk café is open, like my purse,
for constant exploration, myriad
configurations. I fall into a lyric
couch of oxytocin and rehearse
a list of chores that soon gives way to verse
I might put down on paper, were I near it.

Or, in public, finding a friendly spot—
(or at least a place afraid to interfere)
I unhook one side, and introduce the plot
of modesty. Sisters, it makes no sense
this fear of the nipple—standing at the mirror
in a padded bra, searching for offense.

Kathrine Varnes

7.

I GAVE UP PADDED BRAS, certain offense.
I shunned the curve of underwire glam.
Let me be the woman that I am,
I said. Let infants find their milk, the tense
cry of hunger loosen. Impotence
inspired by well-fed babies? Sham.
Shame. Before the press of the mammogram,
let breasts be breasts, whatever audience.

Let breasts be breasts. Our season's brief as is.
It's hard enough to find a bra that fits.
(And those who asked the schoolyard, *Does she stuff?*
now look askance—filled with J. Alfred's fear
a thousand times repeating: *Do I dare?*)
Declare this moment and this peace enough.

Amy Lemmon

Asymptotic

LOVE, TEMPERED BY TIME, pulls to strangle
the little loves it's bred along the way.
It's June again, shot wad of spring, the lair
of promises. Who knows which ones will dangle,
bait for rue, ten years along? Today
he's a straight line and she's a curve, a hair
away from him, never quite touching. Blink
and they're apart—again, almost a couple—
now sharing bites of food across the table,
now sipping cognac, Côtes du Rhône, some drink
that stings. With crème brûlée he swallows trouble:
she'd be his asymptote, too close, unstable,
too sweet-and-sour. Dessert dispatched, they part,
breath held till each is off the other's chart.

Amy Lemmon

Invitation

LOOSEN YOUR TIE, dear sir, admit instead
the mouth I proffer soft along your nape.
The office locked, phone mute, calls forwarded,
let go the herringbone, the oxford's drape.
No words. No sound. Not even a slight nod.
I've read your eyes, taken their rapid shift
to mine in humdrum rooms, dull talk abroad,
dull folks. I've felt our glances hold and lift
above the meeting table just too long
for happenstance. The signal's out. So strong
despite our work, despite our separate rings,
we'd dance and tangle, circus-like. We'd cling.
Yes loosen, do, the armor. Let it fall.
I'll entertain your body's carnival.

Jo Ann Clark

Scheherazade to the King, 10th Anniversary

MUCH WILL HAVE CHANGED since your last visit.
Much else will be almost identical—
in the darkness I mean, in the exquisite
dark. It was never our way to freefall

into *us*. We were pronominally
discrete to the last: *we* alone *I* alone you…
Shall we go on—*she* alone *he*?
Or try something new?

Together would be something
new for us. I'm willing if you're willing
as well. Forget the combination
to this karma-sutran
lock—else embark from the self-same curious
dock: our starting point; our terminus.

Tatyana Mishel

Slut Sonnet III

WE SMELL, I BURN, your knees are at my feet.
A tongue, all muscle, moves me across this pink
shag rug. Slick gore of newborns—how we'll stink!
They'll know, so what, I'll hobble down the street,
flaunt my *oh-shit-I-did-it* limp—tut-tut,
oh, much too young. Three short pumps and you're done.
Not Much, what lurks inside those 501s.
But then you nibble, O'Keeffean treat, a slut
is born. And pain or pleasure? I lose track
when limbs pack tight with yours, and then, flashes:
a girl, a broken tree, rope swing, lake splashes,
it's dusk and late to bed. No going back.
O Sex, the first betrayal, leaving home;
our Mothers fade to strangers with each ripe moan.

Tatyana Mishel

Slut Sonnet IV

So, Moms: Don't fade to strangers. Ripe inside
forgotten *Cosmo's*, past the Do's and Don'ts,
your girls find pages marked with O's—(Oh! *Lies!*
Then why is mother sad?) What if I don't
work quite that way? It's *practice* Madame C
prescribes: the solo prompts and rushing water
as households fill with teens in baths. "Um, gee,"
excuses ring, "I fell asleep." Yawn. Saunter,
babble on through dinner, brother stares. Skip
dessert, bolt to the bedroom, show the mirror
the grown-up skin: the woman's thighs, brown lips,
the righteous pussy. Could there be a better
body part? It must be worshipped. Send in
men, men! We'll take the fucking out of sin.

Rose Kelleher

Hiding

It's loud enough to make the rafters ring,
that *crack!* of hide on hide. They slam together,
beating time, a steady, startling
yin-yang of un-tanned skin and well-tanned leather.

There hides, in such romantic aberrations,
a kind of poetry. Not in the fleshy bounce,
the heat, the sweat, the moans, the undulations,
but their intensity; the way it mounts,

a metaphor whose gentle tenor hides
behind the ruddy face of something else—
something that shares a bloodline, like a brother,

and moves with the same familiar, rhythmic strides,
likened less by the eye than by the pulse—
one act of love that hides inside another.

Rose Kelleher

Rope

Rope burns. It rubs against whatever's tender—
bare ankle bones, the inside of the wrist—
drawn to places where a man is slender
and doelike, like a girl. When you resist,

it hugs you tighter. Don't play hard to get.
Wrestling with it only demonstrates
its power over you: your fear, your sweat,
your straining muscles. Rope insinuates

itself into your weak spots, showing off
your beauty in its own sidewinding way,
reminding us a man is hard and soft;

the way black hair brings out a diamond's luster,
or brushstrokes, with their artful interplay
of smooth and rough, remind us of the master.

Rafael Campo

III. Superman Is Dead

I USED TO THINK that immortality
Was just like Superman, without the tights
And cape—just flying naked through the sky,
As muscled as the clouds, able to leap
Tall buildings in a single bound. I thought
To be invincible was what it meant—
To live forever! I was innocent.
Back then, I hadn't learned the words they taught,
Like hemochromatosis, kryptonite.
And now, I wonder whether words do weigh
Upon the soul. I wonder if I say
Your name urgently enough at night,
Might you descend and hold me in your arms
Again, like Superman but naked, free
And muscled as the clouds, able to leap
Back into bed, your body hard and warm.

Rafael Campo

IX. Your Voice

LAST NIGHT, WHEN WE made love, I saw inside
Your voice, how cavernous it was, and full of wings.
I wandered through it, not quite suffering
But drenched in sweat. Your mouth was magnified,
As was my heart, beyond the size of God,
Beyond the vast red size an open rose
Can grow when held beneath the love-struck nose—
So this is immortality, I said,
With skin and sweat instead of words; my mouth
Was full of you, your voice, your ears, your thighs.
I saw inside your eyes, and mystified
By them, I asked you questions about death.
You answered me with moans, and in your semen
I tasted life, I tasted rain, and then
I brushed my thumb across your dimpled chin
Since you were smiling, rose-voiced, sent from heaven.

Midge Goldberg

Flume Ride

Y%%OUR ARMS SLIDE AROUND MY WAIST%%, and we are going,
and I am pressed full length back into you.
We click and rock heavenward only knowing
the outline of the way but not the view,
the feel of every curve, turning and twisting.
Our fingers intertwine, and gravity
falls before us, leaving us resisting
in a well of weightlessness, then we

are dropping, through loops and lesser hills
of rapids run to overspills,
locked and tumbling together, falling
like eagles plummeting, calling,
until the boat slows, and we are there.
Your fingers comb the water from my hair.

Midge Goldberg

Temptress

APPLES? NO GOOD. If I were going to try
and tempt you, it would be with pecan pie,
sticky and sweet, or steak—filet mignon—
or burnished Irish whiskey, burring on
the tongue, the taste of darkened candlelight.
Besides, an apple's everything that sex
is not—crisp, clean—then there's that whole Snow White
thing happening: the ugly hag, the hex.
Who'd want one after that? But I'll make do;
this apple's what I've got to offer you.
If knowledge is a fruit that men desire,
I'll hold it, out of reach, a little higher.
Perhaps there are times that an apple's right.
Here—I dare you. Know me. Take a bite.

Christopher Bakken

A Concert of Ancient Music, Houston

THOSE WHO THINK ONLY of weakness and pain,
   if they bothered to come here at all,
failed to hear in that homemade salpinx
   the even bleats of twine-hobbled goats.
And those who still believe in sin, who cry
   at pretty epitaphs on despots' tombs
would miss the blatant Neanderthal belch
   of a large double-aulos, would not know
the wailing of island cats in heat,
   or the mildewed cave we share in Oia,
where we improvised our own octaves,
   love, after bottles of resinated wine—
secret hours underground recalled tonight
   by pandouras and the six-holed photinx.

Laura Maffei

The Gambit

Your finger in my ponytail, my dear,
creates a bigger flame than you might guess
a playful gesture could. Before I hear
your footsteps up behind me, you finesse
a mini-violation and I laugh
and want you instantly. And isn't that
the way it starts for us—the half-
approach, the joke, the pouncing like a cat
upon its sister in the rustling grass?
So sudden, yet so mirthful—saving face
in case it might be better just to pass
each other by. But we keep up the chase,
your heated mouth mere inches from my skin,
me holding still to let it all begin.

Lesley Wheeler

Two Swimmers

S̲o̲ ̲s̲u̲r̲e̲ I ̲w̲a̲s̲ ̲y̲o̲u̲'̲d̲ ̲w̲a̲n̲t̲ to have me back
I practiced shining through the intertidal
twilight: eye spots, zebra stripes, empty saddle.
My suckers strained to kiss, my ten arms slack
and cold as the silt plain of my bivouac,
my three hearts wild with yes and weep and puzzle.
An ardent cephalopod unfolds her mantle
onto the rustling currents.
                                        The small waves smack
the great rocks and shiver apart. The stars
beneath are dreaming of the upper glare
and this is the silver film, the glass that thinks
to part them. A human swimmer strokes her ars
poetica along the rim, unaware
she drifts within a mist of anxious ink.

Julie Stoner

Dear John (Drafts 1-4)

~~Dear Bluebeard—Yes, this means I found your cache~~
~~of body parts. You *promised* me, you *swore*,~~
~~and still you're hoarding pornographic trash!~~
~~I'm gone. No need to hide it anymore.~~

~~Dear Dr. Frankenstein—I can't compete~~
~~with patchworked fantasy. My flesh is *real*,~~
~~and therefore flawed. You only want its heat~~
~~to animate your scavenged, fused ideal.~~

~~Dear Don Quijote—Dammit, don't pretend~~
~~I'm Dulcinea! Love me as I *am*,~~
~~not as you *wish* I were! I can't ascend~~
~~that pedestal…nor tolerate this sham.~~

Dear John—This isn't working. You know why.
Go buy yourself a blow-up doll. Goodbye.

A.E. Stallings

Fire Safety Drill

It ought to be easy to learn:
Freeze, drop where you stand,
And roll yourself in a rug;
But acting as you've planned
When the glib tongue licks your hair
Or nibbles up your sleeve
Is difficult—the tug
Of heat unravels thought—
And all that you were taught
Comes brilliantly undone.
And in the moment's flare
Somehow you believe
That it can be outrun,
And you've got time to burn.

A.E. Stallings

The Married Muse

MAYBE IT'S TOO INTIMATE for lovers:
Jostling elbows through the coupled years,
Laundry and dishes, stews salted with tears,
Tossing between the same scratchy covers,
When all conception is the daily grind,
The dawn's alarm, cold shower, black caffeine,
The stare-down of a flat computer screen—
Scraping sonnets out of the skull's rind;

But sometimes I remember it in dreams
Just as consciousness begins to burn—
The utterance that's greater than it seems,
The inspiration that still parts the lips,
The rhythm in the rocking of the hips—
The cycle spins. I iron and I yearn.

Jenny Factor

Learning Stick
1. With Him

Eyeing a dashboard high as the San Gabriels,
I shake that thing, that wiggly bulbous member
back and forth the way he showed me to
and drag it into first and ease one foot,
trading weight and trying to feel cues
to shift, give over. Close to me, his lips
(*Next time put the clutch foot down. Remember.*)
twitch suppression to each start and jerk.
My halting round the block is wincing work
for Man as Mountain, rigid sealed machine.
Arms in a sweat, my heart jazzed, every shove
curses the beast that moves then will not move.
Strained with will-to-please, here is my start:
locked metal box fueled by a nervous heart.

Jenny Factor

2. With Her

HUMIDITY LIFTS US TENSE and intricate,
descanting out on fifteenth-century roads
with names I can't pronounce. Lame rental car
after the automatic one gets towed.
I stretch my legs out in the driver's chair.
She says, *I'll teach you. Yes?* Me here, her there.
Then every nervous motion meets a sound,
her farm-bred coaxing, soothing, settling down—
soon we are sliding over night-sheened stones,
Bruce and Joni on the stereo,
and singing. If I stall once at a toll
as police pull up, and if once more
I stop a workday morning bus' rush—
hey, it's just fine, we girls, we only us.

Jenny Factor

3. With Me

INTO A RHYTHM RULED by *kgrrr* and *bprrrr*,
vibration I am born of, borne by, seated
on the driver's side. The whoosh of heat is
respiration to this solo drive.
Winter ice, the mirroring of road
gives me back my face my face my face,
the sheen of headlights slicing as I brace
my clutch foot with my gear hand in one motion.
Driving's solitary, sealed, devotion
that pounds my thinking into engine grime,
detaching, reattaching, driving time
meets meditation, speeding, shifting, slowed,
responses to my body and the road—
lessons of my life I've learned alone.

Elizabeth M. Johnson

from Open House (a crown*)*

MY FOCUS IS REPLACING you. Most times,
fumbled encounters end at the front door.
But when you took our bed, I bought a Stearns
& Foster; seven grand, king-size, so far
above the floor, to climb in it I use
small stairs. Bought 800-thread-count sheets,
made of Egyptian cotton, and a goose
down-filled duvet. Oasis and retreat;
I've nicknamed it *Venus Man Trap* (although
my best guy friend, who's way too interested
in girl-on-girl, thinks that name aims too low:
Why not the Venus Person Trap instead?
he asks). King Arthur's Court awaits its Lance-
lot. The ballroom's ready for the dance.

Elizabeth M. Johnson

from Open House (a crown)

THE BATHROOM'S READY for romance. It's lit
with candles, and he's filled the tub, turned on
the jets, added bath salts. This room's for *shit*
and *piss*, and *pick* and *clip*, and *tweeze* and *comb*,
minutiae of the day and night. *What if
it's that routine to fall in love*, I think,
for too long I've been making it too tough?
We strip, he pushes me against the sink,
then in the bath. Activity, then still-
ness; afterwards he gently soaps my hair.
Later undoubtedly we'll fuss at all
the water that we've sloshed onto the floor,
but *oh*, I think, *it could be this routine*,
to feel so next to godliness, and clean.

Jill Alexander Essbaum

We Lie Like Poems

WE LIE LIKE POEMS, undulating rhyme.
We stress and then undress to the iamb
of our union. What prosody—the ram's
staff and the ewe's curve, empty, then filled. Line
upon line, we write stanzas. Each nighttime,
images spill from our allegoric limbs
as if water or fire. My skin is hymn
meter in the making, my good song shines
and suffers. Now break me, O Caesura,
I am madrigal, I bear repeating.
Recite me once again. Hark to the muse.
We refrain. We're epic, psalm and saga;
we're sin and synesthesia. The drinking
and weeping's been done. Couplets come in twos.

Jill Alexander Essbaum

Oh We Are Dancing

OH WE ARE DANCING. Oh we undress. Oh
how your hands handle my breasts. I open
like a door, I unhinge. Oh your moistened
lips limping up the well-traveled road
of my thighbone. Oh the reddening rose
and her mystery bliss. She groans, she glistens.
Oh she listens. Speak tongues, Thou Great Physician,
heal my deepening need. Oh memento,
remember this: *not for my skin and all*
its sinning shall I ever dare repent.
Oh forbidden, I am wicked but prohibit my taboo.
Oh swollen, I'm engorged. Oh waterfall,
I'm drenched. Oh Father, forgive. I know not
who I do. Oh beast. Oh bastard. *Oh you.*

Jill Alexander Essbaum

I Swanned

I SWANNED AT THE GOLD calf's hoof, I whored
to the rosebud's burning bush. In the sanctuary,
even, praying like an apostate Mary
with my hands beneath my dress. Have you bored
of me, Lord? Have you forgotten? Therefore,
let me remind you: with a temptingly
empty mouth, I knelt before you, worthy
as water, wet as wine. And I poured
myself out, and you swallowed me up. Christ,
our unknown hour comes thirty years too late.
Inadequate, my sacrifice. Reckless,
my display. I prostrated my crevice,
my creed. I was your slave, your novitiate.
How I hoped like a heathen for holiness.

Randall Mann

The Church Militant

My mouth trembling was a sign of something bad.
I did not believe I could be healed with prayers.
I took the liberty to tell past sins to others.
In distress, have I often wished I were dead?

When my eyebrow twitches, it is not a sign of evil.
I have delighted in lewd signals and afterwards
put them into practice. I have said suggestive words.
My desires have been intricate and carnal.

Speaking with an older boy, or embracing,
was I aroused? I have had intercourse with another;
as you say, he investigated me from behind. But did

I consummate the act? I have gone around trying
to do this. I have been both the procurer
and the procuress. I have often wished I were dead.

Randall Mann

Uncle

OH, THESE OLD WEEDS? The heels are come hither,
But with balance. Still, my black pants,
I know, make my ass look like Yoko's,
That cover of *Double Fantasy*, holy flapjacks!
Uncle enjoyed a hearty meal, the diversity of syrup
At IHOP. Somehow we always ended up there,
Rearranging the filthy dahlias.
You, with your nose in the Splenda:

Now's not the time for grief: he *was*
Old, in cat years. (Instead, I like to think of that one
Tweaked-out morn we were ordered to leave the baths.)
Irenic to the end, he held up his last
Cocktail (awful stuff) and said, rather like
Edmund White, "To all my tricks."

Carol Quinn

After Tsvetaeva and Mandelstam at the Kremlin Cathedral

EACH DOME SUPPORTS ANOTHER. One leans against
the other (as the golden shells inhere)—
and these lovers must have walked here once:
a young Derzhavin and his Aurora in fur.

Each church kept separate hours. Bells relayed
the lingering moment in polyphonies.
A choir felt their voices catch, delayed
within a cupola: a madrigal's slow chase.

How young the singers were. It would not last—
but *a cappella*, both could still recall
their old harmonic parts—though words were lost—
and sing as if such songs would keep them whole.

And after years and wars and other loves,
the words would fall like snow on unmarked graves.

Quincy R. Lehr

We All Have Our Needs

I WATCH TWO TWENTYSOMETHINGS on the train
and know what's on their minds, their faces stuck
in cautious non-expression as their brains
grow giddy with their unexpected luck.
But why suppress their feelings? There's no shame
in wanting it, in getting some at last,
a little closer with each station passed—
a gonad's urge that no one needs to name.

But when you score, something always slips
from balled-up sheets, from minds, from frenzied lips.
And past the press of chests and groins and hair
a silence settles—trumping everything
that you can say, or hold to, even cling
against yourself—and saturates the air.

Jessica Piazza

Ankylophobia: *Fear of immobility of a joint*

LOCKED HERE, I'M LOCH-JAWED: a Nessie of
tetanus. Unhook me, unhinge me, this
liquid imprisonment. Taciturn
elbow, mulish talocrural, my
stubbornest joint is submerged in your
tallow. This candle, this window, you
squirm like a minnow, repeat like an
echo, arthritic libido. I'm
caught. I'm unmovable. Abjectly
literal. You? Irresistible
force meeting object, we forge into
junction—one tongue in one groove, and we
fit, ad infinitum. Limit my
movement. I'll ease your impediment.

Jessica Piazza

Apodysophilia: *Love of undressing*

WHEN MANY VEILS are pared to one what more
to gain obscured? The dance must end. One spin:
the veil has fallen to the floor. One more:
the centrifuge that I become has pinned
you there. Again, I win. Undone, my clasp
has claws. This sloughing of my clothes breaks laws
that aren't written yet. And now my grasp
is masquerading as embrace because
many a lip twixt cup and slip have tried
to bare my cloth-clad heart. But what I hide
is hidden even more the more I show.
Still, all of this means *yes*. The air's desired
caress; I have no *no*. You're sure you know
me, so? You've guessed. There's nothing to undress.

Sandra Beasley

from Chronic Medea
VII. Husband. Wife.

In here I own the voyage of your hip,
the rip and sway of skin commanding skin:
Here. Hard. The borders between us so thin
my words pledge their allegiance to your lip.

But then this bedroom door yields to a ship
with crew that mutters underneath my feet.
A kitchen down below the wife must keep,
while husband counts the stars and charts the trip.

For twenty years I've plagued all men with loves
and thought them weak. I've quartered hearts to trick
up soups, asphyxiated with a kiss.
One winter, caught two cooing turtledoves,
knit a scarf of fresh entrails. Love, let's stick
to lust. I've got the recipes for this.

Mela Kirkpatrick

Gaea

HE SCOOPED UNHURRIED FINGERS through her hair
and watched the sifting strands slip loose, and fall,
and fan onto the linen sheets, till all
lay shining, as sometimes in the market square
he wandered through the merchants' many lanes
to find that siren stall, its baskets filled
with rices, lentils, for his fingers thrilled
to delve, to feel the cadence of the grains.

She shifted under him and watched the gold
within his eyes, her falling hair, his hands,
the way the body intensifies a thirst,
and sensed a calling in herself, that old
and sweet desire by which the world expands:
to be the texture, nutrient, and earth.

Chloe Haralambous

Circe's Loom

At midnight, Circe's man blacks out, her fix
Kicks in, she takes her glass to the loom and taps
The stiletto rhythm of Friday night; the tricks
Of fur-clad blondes who break from suburban flats.
The sharp-toothed tabloid brides of crimson blues
And coral handcuffs (handfucks?) head (tail)
To jazz-packed axes of smoke and frothing booze;
Forlorn boys' aches for stockinged calves and veil-
Draped breasts; the drooling dreams of woven sheets
That cling to cheeks like lips to teeth; the blow
Of sibyls' eyelids. Mink-warm talons beat
On poor boys' palms, they follow their lamias home.
Suburban flats light up with woven dreams.
Spent Circe yawns, packs up her purple weavings.

CONTRIBUTORS

Kim Addonizio's latest books are *Ordinary Genius: A Guide for the Poet Within* and *Lucifer at the Starlite*. Her collection *Tell Me* was a National Book Award Finalist. Addonizio's honors include two NEA Fellowships, a Guggenheim, and a Pushcart Prize. Her other books include the novels *Little Beauties* and *My Dreams Out in the Street*. www.kimaddonizio.com.

Christopher Bakken is the author of two books of poetry: *Goat Funeral* (2006) and *After Greece* (2001), for which he received the T.S. Eliot Prize in poetry. He is also co-translator of *The Lions' Gate: Selected Poems of Titos Patrikios*. He teaches at Allegheny College in Pennsylvania.

Tony Barnstone, the Albert Upton Professor of English at Whittier College, is author of four books of poetry, five translations from Chinese, and three textbooks. Awards: NEA, California Arts Council, Pushcart, Grand Prize of the Strokestown International Poetry Festival (Ireland), Benjamin Saltman Award in Poetry, John Ciardi Prize in Poetry.

Willis Barnstone is an American poet, memoirist, translator, Hispanist, and comparatist. He has translated the Ancient Greek poets and the complete fragments of the pre-Socratic philosopher Heraclitus. A Guggenheim fellow, he has four times been nominated for the Pulitzer Prize in Poetry and has had four Book of the Month Club selections.

Sandra Beasley won the 2009 Barnard Women Poets Prize for *I Was the Jukebox*, selected by Joy Harjo and published by W. W. Norton. Her first collection, *Theories of Falling*, won the

2007 New Issues Poetry Prize judged by Marie Howe. She lives in Washington, D.C.

Kate Bernadette Benedict, of New York City, is the author of two full-length poetry collections, *Here from Away* (2003) and *In Company* (2011). She edits the online poetry journals *Umbrella*, *Bumbershoot*, and *Tilt-a-Whirl*. For many years she was a moderator at *Eratosphere*, the online poetry forum.

David Bergman is the author of *Heroic Measures* and *Cracking the Code*, which won the George Elliston Prize. With Katia Sainson, he translated *The Selected Poems of Jean Senac*. He has written two critical books, *Gaiety Transfigured* and *The Violet Hour: The Violet Quill and the Making of Gay Culture*.

Meredith Bergmann is a sculptor who works both on public monuments and on a private scale. Her largest public commission has been for the Boston Women's Memorial. Pictures of her work may be seen at www.meredithbergmann.com. She is the poetry editor of the *American Arts Quarterly* and its related website: www.nccsc.net/poetry.

John Berryman (1914-1972) was the author of numerous poetry collections and several works of prose. His book, *77 Dream Songs*, was published in 1964 and awarded a Pulitzer Prize. He was elected a Fellow of The Academy of American Poets in 1966 and served as a Chancellor from 1968 until his death.

Rafael Campo teaches and practices general internal medicine at Harvard Medical School and Beth Israel Deaconess Medical Center in Boston, where his medical practice serves mostly Latinos, gay/lesbian/bisexual/transgendered people, and people with HIV infection. He is also on the faculty of the Lesley University Creative Writing MFA program. The author of numerous award-winning books of poetry and essays, he has received a John Simon Guggenheim Foundation fellowship, and he is a recipient of both the Annual Achievement Award from the National Hispanic Academy of Arts and Sciences and a Pushcart Prize.

Michael Cantor's work has appeared in *The Dark Horse, Measure, The Atlanta Review, Raintown Review, Margie, Chimaera* and numerous other journals and anthologies. Honors include the New England Poetry Club Erika Mumford (2006) and Gretchen Warren (2008) Prizes. A chapbook, *The Performer*, was published by Pudding House Press in 2007.

Hayden Carruth (1921-2008), author of more than thirty books of poetry, several prose collections, and a novel, was honored during his lifetime with awards from the Bollingen Foundation, the Guggenheim Foundation, and the National Endowment for the Arts, and a 1995 Lannan Literary Fellowship. He also won the Lenore Marshall Award, the Paterson Poetry Prize, the Vermont Governor's Medal, the Carl Sandburg Award, the Whiting Award, and the Ruth Lilly Prize, among many others.

Grace Cavalieri is author of several books of poems and produced plays. The latest book is *Sounds Like Something I Would Say* (2010, Casa Menendez). Her forthcoming play is *Anna Nicole: Blonde Ambition*. She founded and still produces public radio's "The Poet and the Poem," now from the Library of Congress, celebrating more than 33 years on-air.

Jo Ann Clark earned an MFA in Writing from Columbia University and has taught literature and workshops at schools in Rome, at The School of the Art Institute of Chicago, and at Bank Street College in Manhattan. Her translations of the Russian poet, Anna Akhmatova, have been featured in *The Paris Review*.

Maryann Corbett is the author of two chapbooks: *Dissonance* (Scienter Press, 2009) and *Gardening in a Time of War* (Pudding House, 2007). Her poems, essays, and translations have appeared in more than sixty journals in print and online, including *River Styx, Atlanta Review, The Dark Horse*, and *The Evansville Review*.

"Wesli Court" is the anagram pseudonym under which Lewis Turco, author of *The Book of Forms: A Handbook of Poetics*, writes his traditionally formal verse. His most recent book is *The Gathering of the Elders and Other Poems*, ww.StarCloudPress.com, 2010. *The Collected Lyrics of Lewis Turco / Wesli Court 1953-2004* appeared from Star Cloud in 2004.

e.e. cummings (1894-1962), author of numerous collections of poetry and two volumes of prose, received many honors during his lifetime, including an Academy of American Poets Fellowship, two Guggenheim Fellowships, the Charles Eliot Norton Professorship at Harvard, the Bollingen Prize in Poetry in 1958, and a Ford Foundation grant.

Robert W. Crawford lives in Derry, NH. His poem "The Empty Chair" won the 2006 Howard Nemerov Sonnet Award. His first book of poetry, *Too Much Explanation Can Ruin a Man*, was published in 2005. He is a trustee of the Robert Frost Farm in Derry, and a member of the Powow River Poets.

Tim Dlugos (1950-1990) was a prominent younger poet who was active in both the Mass Transit poetry scene in Washington, DC in the early 1970s and New York's downtown literary scene in the late seventies and eighties. He died of AIDS on December 3, 1990. *A Fast Life: The Collected Poems of Tim Dlugos*, edited by David Trinidad, is forthcoming from Nightboat Books.

Sharon Dolin's fourth book, *Burn and Dodge* (University of Pittsburgh Press, 2008) won the AWP Donald Hall Prize in Poetry. Recent winner of a Pushcart Prize (2011), she is Writer-in-Residence at Eugene Lang College, The New School and also teaches at the Unterberg Poetry Center of the 92nd Street Y.

Moira Egan's poetry collections are *Cleave; La Seta della Cravatta/The Silk of the Tie; Bar Napkin Sonnets;* and *Spin* (Entasis Press, 2010). A firm believer in the relevance of the sonnet, she is currently working on her next series, *Hot Flash Sonnets*. She lives in Rome with her husband/translator, Damiano Abeni.

Jill Alexander Essbaum's most recent publications include *Harlot* (No Tell Books, 2007), *Necropolis* (NeoNuma Arts, 2008), and *The Devastation* (Cooper Dillon Books, 2009). She lives in Austin, TX.

Jenny Factor's first book, *Unraveling at the Name* (Copper Canyon Press) won a Hayden Carruth Award and was a finalist for the Lambda Literary Award. Jenny received her BA from Harvard College. She currently serves as Core Faculty in Poetry at Antioch University Los Angeles's low-residency MFA program.

Midge Goldberg's poems have appeared in *Measure, First Things, Alehouse 2008, Cadenza, Poetry Speaks Who I Am*, and other publications. She was a finalist for the 2008 Nemerov Sonnet Award. Her first book of poetry, *Flume Ride*, was published in 2006 by David Robert Books. She lives in Derry, NH.

Thom Gunn (1929-2004) published numerous collections of poetry and a book of essays; his collection *The Man with the Night Sweats* received the Lenore Marshall Poetry Prize in 1993. His many honors include the Levinson Prize, an Arts Council of Great Britain Award, a Rockefeller Award, the PEN (Los Angeles) Prize for Poetry, the Sara Teasdale Prize, a Lila Wallace-Reader's Digest Award, the Forward Prize, and fellowships from the Guggenheim and MacArthur Foundations.

Marilyn Hacker is the author of twelve books of poems, including *Names* (W.W. Norton, 2009), *Essays on Departure* (Carcanet Press, UK, 2006) and *Desesperanto* (W.W. Norton, 2003). Her essay collection *Unauthorized Voices* was published by the University of Michigan Press in 2010. Her ten volumes of translations from the French include Marie Étienne's *King of a Hundred Horsemen* (Farrar, Straus and Giroux, 2008), which received the 2007 Robert Fagles Translation Prize and the 2009 American PEN Award for Poetry in Translation; and Vénus Khoury-Ghata's *Nettles* (The Graywolf Press, 2008). For her own work, she is a past recipient of the Lenore Marshall Award, the Poets' Prize, the National Book Award, two Lambda Literary Awards, and the American PEN Voelcker Award for poetry in 2010. She is a Chancellor of the Academy of American Poets.

Chloe Haralambous was born in Rome, where she grew up speaking English, Greek, and Italian. She studied poetry with

Moira Egan and twice won the Keats-Shelley Memorial House Poetry Prize. Currently she is a student at Columbia University, where, when not writing papers, she continues to write poems.

Clarinda Harriss, Professor Emerita of English at Towson University, is the author of six poetry collections, most recently *Air Travel*, *Dirty Blue Voice*, and *Mortmain*. Her poems appear in such magazines as *Poetry*, *Smartish Pace*, *Prairie Schooner*, and *Texas Quarterly* and have been widely anthologized. Her textbook, *Forms of Verse: British and American*, has been in continuous classroom use since its publication in the mid-1970s. She directs BrickHouse Books, Inc., Maryland's oldest literary press.

H.L. Hix teaches in the creative writing MFA program at the University of Wyoming. His most recent book, *First Fire, Then Birds: Obsessionals 1985-2010*, was published in September 2010 by Etruscan Press. His website is www.hlhix.com.

Elizabeth M. Johnson is an attorney who specializes in commercial litigation. She lives in Chicago, IL.

Julie Kane won first prize in the 2007 Open Poetry International Sonnet Competition. Her two most recent poetry collections are *Jazz Funeral* (2009), David Mason's choice for the Donald Justice Poetry Prize, and *Rhythm & Booze* (2003), Maxine Kumin's selection for the National Poetry Series and a Poets' Prize finalist. She teaches at Northwestern State University in Natchitoches, Louisiana.

Rose Kelleher's first book, *Bundle o' Tinder*, was selected by Richard Wilbur for the 2007 Anthony Hecht Poetry Prize. She is fantastically hot. That is, hot only in her fantasies.

Mela Kirkpatrick is currently an instructor in the Writing Seminars at Johns Hopkins University, where she received her MFA in 2010. She studied art history and creative writing at UNC-Chapel Hill. Her poems have been published in *Agenda*, *The Carolina Quarterly*, *Dappled Things*, and *Measure*.

David W. Landrum teaches English at Grand Valley State University, in Allendale, Michigan. His poetry has appeared in numerous publications; his sonnets have appeared in *14 by 14*, *Umbrella*, *The New Formalist*, *Trinacria*, and many other on-line and print magazines.

David Lehman's latest books are *Yeshiva Boys*, a collection of poems (Scribner), and *A Fine Romance: Jewish Songwriters, American Songs* (Nextbook/Schocken). He is the editor of *The Oxford Book of American Poetry* and the series editor of *The Best American Poetry*. He teaches in the graduate writing program of the New School in New York City.

Quincy R. Lehr is the author of two collections, *Across the Grid of Streets* and *Obscure Classics of English Progressive Rock*, and is the associate editor of *The Raintown Review*. His work has appeared widely in the U.S., UK, Ireland, Australia, and the Czech Republic. He lives in Brooklyn.

Amy Lemmon is the author of *Fine Motor* (Sow's Ear Poetry Review Press, 2008) and *Saint Nobody* (Red Hen Press, 2009) and coauthor, with Denise Duhamel, of *ABBA: The Poems* (Coconut Books, 2010) and *Enjoy Hot or Iced: Poems in Conversation* (Slapering Hol Press, 2011). She is an associate professor of English at New York's Fashion Institute of Technology.

Laura Maffei is the author of *Drops from Her Umbrella*

Acknowledgments

Kim Addonizio: "Stolen Moments", "So What", from *What Is This Thing Called Love: Poems By Kim Addonizio*. Copyright © 2004 by Kim Addonizio. Used by permission of W.W. Norton & Company, Inc. "First Poem For You" first appeared in *The Philosopher's Club*, Boa Editions, © 1994 by Kim Addonizio and is reprinted with the permission of the author.

Christopher Bakken: "A Concert of Ancient Music, Houston" appeared in *After Greece* (Truman State University Press, 2001).

Willis Barnstone: "With a French Nun in Lapland": *The Secret Reader: 501 Sonnets*, University Press of New England, 1996, Copyright © Willis Barnstone.

Sandra Beasley: "Husband. Wife" from the "Chronic Medea" sequence, part of a selection of poems that won the 2006 Elinor Benedict Poetry Prize from *Passages North*, appears with the permission of the author.

Kate Bernadette Benedict, "Celibate Observances" was originally published in *Here from Away* (CW Books, 2003); reprinted with permission of the author.

John Berryman: sonnet #1 "I wished, all the mild days of middle March" and sonnet #4 "Ah when you drift hover before you kiss" from "Sonnets To Chris" from *Collected Poems: 1937-1971 by John Berryman.* © 1989 by Kate Donahue Berryman. Reprinted by permission of Farrar, Straus and Giroux, LLC.

Rafael Campo: "The Immortal Song: III" and "Superman Is Dead" from *What the Body Told*, Rafael Campo. Copyright © 1996, Rafael Campo. All rights reserved. Reprinted by permission of the publisher, Duke University Press.

Michael Cantor: "The Love of Sushi Sue" was originally published in *Medicinal Purposes*.

Hayden Carruth, "Sonnet 9" ("To see a woman long oppressed by fear") from *Collected Shorter Poems 1946-1991*. Copyright © 1989, 1992 by Hayden Carruth. Reprinted with the permission of Copper Canyon Press, www.coppercanyonpress.org.

Maryann Corbett: "Rose Catalogue In January" was published in *Chronicles*, March 2010.

e.e. cummings: "after your poppied hair inaugurates". Copyright © 1973, 1983, 1991 by the Trustees for the e. e. cummings Trust. Copyright © 1973, 1983 by George James Firmage. "and this day is was spring...us". Copyright 1923, 1925, 1951, 1953, © 1991 by the Trustees for the e. e. cummings Trust. Copyright © 1976 by George James Firmage, from *Erotic Poems By E.E. Cummings*, edited by George James Firmage. Used by permission of Liveright Publishing Corporation.

Tim Dlugos: "Sonnet" and "Spy of Love" originally appeared in *The James White Review* (Vol. 17, No. 2; spring 2000). Copyright © 2000 by the Estate of Tim Dlugos. Reprinted by permission.

Sharon Dolin: "Wanting Two: A Sonnet/Ghazal" from *Burn*

And Dodge, by Sharon Dolin, © 2008. Reprinted by permission of the University Of Pittsburgh Press. "Now That I Have Lain With You" is printed with the permission of the author.

Moira Egan: "With A Line From Millay" and "Millay Goes Down" first appeared in *Prairie Schooner*, then in *Best American Poetry 2008* (Edited by Charles Wright; Series Editor David Lehman); they also appear in *Spin* (Entasis Press, 2010) and are reprinted with permission of the author. "Variation and quick change" appeared in *The Same*. "On Hot Sonnets" found its start as "Sex and the Sonnet," first published in the *Shit Creek Review*.

Jill Alexander Essbaum: "We," "Oh We," and "I" from the chapbook *Oh Forbidden* (2005 Pecan Grove Press).

Jenny Factor: "Learning Stick" from *Unraveling At The Name*. Copyright © 2002 By Jenny Factor. Reprinted with the permission of Copper Canyon Press. www.coppercanyonpress.org.

Midge Goldberg: "Flume Ride" was published in *Dogwood*, and "Temptress" was published in *Mezzo Cammin*.

Thom Gunn: "Diagrams" from *Collected Poems* by Thom Gunn. Copyright © 1994 by Thom Gunn. Reprinted by permission of Farrar, Straus and Giroux, LLC.

Marilyn Hacker: "Aglow in the summer evening, a desk-lamp's yellow" from "Scars On Paper," from *Squares And Courtyards* by Marilyn Hacker. Copyright © 2000 by Marilyn Hacker. Used by permission of W. W. Norton & Company, Inc. "Future Conditional" and "Symbiose II" From *Love*,

Death, and the Changing of the Seasons, Copyright © 1986 by Marilyn Hacker. Used by permission of the author.

H.L. Hix: "I Will Start by Telling You an Ancient Legend," "As Though the Weather Were Bad in the World of Sexuality," and "This Morally Neutralized Domain of Intercourse" first appeared in *Perfect Hell* (Gibbs Smith, 1996). Reprinted with permission of the author.

Elizabeth M. Johnson: "My Focus" and "The Bathroom" were previously published in *Mezzo Cammin* as part of a sonnet crown entitled "Open House."

Julie Kane: "Finale" was originally published online in *14x14: The Lean Sonnet Zine*, issue 3 (April 2008), and was then reprinted in *Jazz Funeral* (Story Line Press, 2009).

Rose Kelleher: "Rope" and "Hiding" appeared in *32 Poems* and *River Styx*, respectively.

Mela Kirkpatrick: "Gaea" appeared in *Measure*.

David Lehman: "To Summer" (first published online in Nerve.com) and "Split" appear with the permission of the author.

Quincy R. Lehr: "We All Have Our Needs"" first appeared in *Galway First,* having won the Tigh Neachtains Love Sonnet Contest in 2008. It will also appear in *Obscure Classics Of English Progressive Rock*, due out in 2011.

Amy Lemmon: "Asymptotic" appeared in *Enjoy Hot or Iced: Poems in Conversation and a Conversation* (Denise Duhamel and Amy Lemmon), Slapering Hol Press, 2011.

Laura Maffei: "The Gambit" previously appeared in *Measure*.

Randall Mann: "The Church Militant" first appeared in *Complaint In The Garden* (Zoo Press 2004) and appears by permission of the author; "Uncle" appears with permission of the author.

Susan Mclean: "Dark Shadows" was previously published in *Slant*, and it appeared in *The Best Disguise* (University of Evansville Press, 2009).

Mary Meriam: "Melon Balls" was first published in *Sixty-Six: The Journal Of Sonnet Studies*.

Edna St. Vincent Millay: The poems of Edna St. Vincent Millay ("I too beneath your moon, almighty Sex" © 1939, 1967; "I, being born a woman and distressed" © 1923, 1951; "When we are old and these rejoicing veins" © 1931, 1958) by Edna St. Vincent Millay and Norma Millay Ellis. Reprinted by permission of Elizabeth Barnett and Holly Peppe, Literary Executors, The Millay Society.

Leslie Monsour: "At The Summer Poetry Festival" was published in *The Chimaera*.

Molly Peacock: "Couple Sharing A Peach" Copyright © 2002 by Molly Peacock. "Have You Ever Faked An Orgasm?" (Copyright © 1995 By Molly Peacock) and "I Consider The Possibility" (Copyright © 1995 By Molly Peacock) from *Cornucopia: New And Selected Poems By Molly Peacock*. Used by permission of W.W. Norton & Company, Inc.

Jessica Piazza: "Ankylophobia" was originally published in *Pebble Lake Review*; "Apodysophilia" was originally published in *Barrelhouse*.

Carol Quinn: "After Tsvetaeva and Mandelstam" first appeared in *Open Windows 2005* (Anthology, Ghost Road Press) and then in *Acetylene* (2008 Cider Press Review Book Award winner). Reprinted with the permission of the author.

Michael Salcman: "The Sulfurous Days of Summer" appeared in *Loch Raven Review*.

Marilyn L. Taylor: "The Seven Very Liberal Arts" was originally published as a fine letterpress limited edition of the same name by Aralia Press.

David Trinidad: "At the Glass Onion, 1971" is reprinted from *Answer Song* by David Trinidad (High Risk Books, 1994). Copyright © 1994 by David Trinidad. Reprinted by permission of the author.

Wendy Videlock: "Prufrock Takes A Formal Lover" first appeared in *Smartish Pace*.

Lesley Wheeler: "Two Swimmers" was first published in *Prairie Schooner* as part of a collaborative sequence called "Intertidal"; the first line is the last line from the previous sonnet by Kathrine Varnes. It also appeared in *Heathen* (C&R Press, 2009).

Terri Witek: "Edith Sitwell And The Carnal World" first appeared in *American Poetry Review*, then in *Carnal World* (Story Line Press, 2005).